PAM GEMS

Plays Three

PAM GEMS

Plays Three

GO WEST YOUNG WOMAN

KING LUDWIG OF BAVARIA

NELSON

NOT JOAN THE MUSICAL

QUOTA BOOKS LTD
LONDON

First published in 2021 by Quota Books Ltd. 197 Hammersmith Grove, London W6 0NP

website: www.quotabooks.com – *email*: info@quotabooks.com
Twitter: @Quotabooks

Copyright © Pam Gems

Pam Gems is hereby identified as the Author of the Work in accordance with Section 7 of the Copyright, Designs and Patents Act 1988. The author has asserted her moral rights.

All rights whatsoever in these plays are strictly reserved and application for performance etc. should be made before commencement of rehearsals to Rose Cobbe, United Agents, 12-26 Lexington Street, London W1F 0LE, UK. info@unitedagents.co.uk Tel: +44 (0) 20 3214 0800.
No performance may be given unless a licence has been obtained.

This book is sold subject to the condition that it shall not, by way of trade or otherwise, be lent, resold, hired out, or otherwise circulated without the publisher's prior consent in any form of binding or cover other than that in which it is published and without a similar condition, including this condition, being imposed on the subsequent publisher.

A CIP record for this book is available from the British Library.

ISBN 978-1-9162460-9-6

Typeset in the UK by M Rules
Printed and bound by Biddles
Picture of Pam Gems courtesy of Jonathan Gems
Cover design: TRISTAN

Available from Amazon, Ingram Spark, Quota Books
and all politically correct bookstores.

Pam Gems was born in 1925 in Mudeford, near Christchurch, in what was then Dorset, on the south coast of England. Her father, a Welsh ex-coalminer, died when she was six years old, leaving her mother to bring up Pam and her two brothers on her own.

For most of her childhood Pam's family lived in poverty, relying on charity from the parish church and the Salvation Army. At eleven, she won a scholarship to grammar school, where she excelled but left at fifteen to go to work.

World War Two broke out and, in 1943, when she turned eighteen, she joined the Women's Royal Naval Service, and worked with British and Canadian bomber squadrons. After the war, she took up a government scheme providing further education, and went to Manchester University, where she studied psychology and met her future husband.

Always stage-struck, Pam Gems wrote her first play when she was eight, and was an enthusiastic participant in school plays. At university, she joined the dramatic society, wrote skits, produced and directed. After university, she got a job in audience research at the BBC, which she loathed – but enjoyed being part of a London bohemian scene that included Ted Hughes, the poet, and Robert Bolt the playwright.

After marrying and having her first two children, she moved to Wandsworth in South London, with her husband Keith, and started writing radio plays. This began an extraordinarily prolific writing career that produced over seventy plays and adaptations, many of them performed internationally.

Pam Gems is Britain's greatest female playwright, with only Agatha Christie having had more West End productions.

ALSO BY THE SAME AUTHOR

Betty's Wonderful Christmas
Dusa, Fish, Stas and Vi
Queen Christina
Piaf
Aunt Mary
Camille
Loving Women
Pasionaria
Deborah's Daughter
Marlene
Stanley
The Snow Palace
Mrs. Pat
Ethel Merman
Natalya
The Socialists
At the Window

Franz Into April
The Little Mermaid
After Birthday
Up In Sweden
Next Please
Franz Into April
My Warren
The Amiable Courtship of Miz Venus and Wild Bill
The Synonym
The Whippet
The Russian Princess
The Burning Man
A Builder by Trade
The Nourishing Lie
Mr Watts In Donegal
Cluster

Down West
The Country House Sale
In The Hothouse
Ladybird, Ladybird
Ebba
Guin for Guinevere
Marine
Who Is Sylvia?
You Should Be Pleased He Likes Me
What Luck
An Ordinary Woman
Cedric and Louise
The Incorruptible
Garibaldi, si!
The Treat

ADAPTATIONS

The Blue Angel
Sarah B Divine!
My Name is Rosa Luxemburg
Rivers and Forests
Cheri

Uncle Vanya
A Doll's House
The Seagull
Ghosts
Yerma
The Lady from the Sea

The Cherry Orchard
Dance of Death
The Father
Hedda Gabbler
Three Sisters

NOVELS

Mrs Frampton
Bon Voyage, Mrs Frampton

CONTENTS

GO WEST YOUNG WOMAN	1
KING LUDWIG OF BAVARIA	91
NELSON	175
NOT JOAN THE MUSICAL	273

Womens Company

GO WEST YOUNG WOMAN

by pam gems

11 - 15 june, 1974.

The Round House

Chalk Farm Road London NW1 8BG   Box office 01-267 2564

GO WEST YOUNG WOMAN

For Sue Todd and Ann Mitchell

GO WEST YOUNG WOMAN was first performed at the Round House, Camden, London, UK, on 6– 27 June, 1974. Presented by The Women's Theatre Company, co-founded by Pam Gems.

CAST

(in alphabetical order)

STUART BARREN
KATE BESWICK
MALCOLM BULLIVANT
MARGI CAMPI
HELEN DOWNING
RON FORFAR
PATRICIA FRANKLIN
THEA RANFT
JONINA SCOTT
ELLEN SHEEAN
DON WARRINGTON
Directed by SUE TODD and ANN MITCHELL
Designed by SARAH PAULLEY
Music by BOBBY CAMPBELL and TOM PALEY.
Production Assistant BUZZ GOODBODY
Stage Manager CLAIRE HIGNEY
Assistant Stage Manager SARA GEMS

REVIEW

"The play is informative and entertaining rather than proselytizing. Not that there's not a message, but it isn't hard-sell. It is an attempt, simply, to get away from the romantic, movie-inspired, image of the Western woman, which casts them all as Calamity Jane or Annie Get Your Gun, or the sweet innocent daughter of the ranch.

The action is hung on a family's journey out West and the tribulations and transformations they suffer enroute. The message, says Sue Todd, the director, is that the battle for liberation has to be fought incessantly. When the women have battled across the wilderness and arrived in the promised land, they discover that things are just the same. The old problems and systems reassert themselves. They haven't made it. It just ain't that simple. "What happens now?" is the curtain-closing line from the show."

Suzanne Lowry. *The Guardian*. June 7th 1974

GO WEST YOUNG WOMAN

CHARACTERS

JOSIAH WEEKS
EMMA WEEKS
ANNIE WEEKS
LIZZIE WEEKS
MRS CARLTON
OLAF
ERIKA
MISS AMY, THE DRESSMAKER
ETHAN AMES, THE TRAILMASTER
MRS DOLAN
FRANCES DOLAN
MRS CARMODY
MRS DE WITT
MR DE WITT
LOLA BOOLAY
PIECES
VERA
MAC
MANDA
MISS DORA
SNAKE-OIL SALESMAN
INDIAN
CHIEF WHITE CLOUD
INDIAN SQUAW
WATANYE
RED EAGLE
DULL KNIFE
INDIAN SCOUT
CATHERINE BEECHER
ASA MERCER
PREACHER

JIM MCCOURT
LEWIS
ARCHER BURNETT
ARCHER BURNETT'S WIFE
MISS KITTY
ROCKY
STOREMAN
STENOGRAPHER
EMIGRANT WOMEN
OLD-TIMER
UNION SOLDIER
GENERAL CARLTON
ARMY AGENT
COLONEL
COLONEL'S WIFE
OVERSEER
IMMIGRANT GIRL
MRS BLAKE

The play can be performed with seven women, six men, and two ASMs.

GO WEST YOUNG WOMAN

ACT ONE

ACT ONE – SCENE ONE

The Great Plains. A tall INDIAN, standing wrapped in a blanket. The sun is setting.

>   INDIAN
> Ohh ... Ahh ... Eeeeee ... Great Spirit ... let my voice
> rise up to you. All things are thine; the wings of the
> air, and the beasts, and all green things that live.
> Oh, Great Spirit, the Crow country is a good country.
> The air is sweet, the grasses are fresh, and bright
> streams flow out of the snowbanks. You give us the
> elk, the deer, the antelope, and our buffalo are fine
> and large. You give us cottonwood bark for our horses,
> and the cool air of high places. Preserve us, oh great
> Grandfather, from all enemies. Make the rivers
> free from rocks for our canoes to pass. Let not wild
> animals molest the holy places of our dead. Bless for
> us the oak trees that thrive on the winter's storm,
> the summer's heat. Make me strong, like the oak. I
> give worship for the mysteries of light, by which the
> earth and all living things are moved. I give worship
> for the mysteries of darkness and the great bodies of
> the upper world that travel without hindrance. Oh,
> beloved Father, accept my worship and the gifts of
> my heart. There is no place like the Crow country. Oh,
> Great Spirit ... Ohh ... Ahh ... Eeeeee ...

ACT ONE SCENE TWO

EMMA, the mother of two grown daughters (ANNIE and LIZZIE) and a well-dressed guest, MRS CARLTON, are having a tea party.

LIZZIE

Annie and I are so excited!

ANNIE

We can hardly wait to be off... I intend to horse-ride!

EMMA

Hush, girls! Your father hasn't agreed to that. We must see what kind of figure you intend to cut.

ANNIE

I hear the women in the West ride the way men do – in pants!

MRS CARLTON

Oh yes, with an overdress, of course. It's a little strange, but you get used to the sight.

ANNIE

Lizzie wants to marry a soldier – maybe one of Custer's brave lads.

LIZZIE

Can you imagine it, life on the frontier?

ANNIE

Space. Freedom... all around you...

EMMA

Girls, girls! *(To MRS CARLTON)* They've been getting so restless lately.

ACT ONE

LIZZIE

Because Pa won't let us take up anything!

ANNIE

That's why.

EMMA

And the answer is still no. I will not have you renting yourselves out in paid work. Your father would never live it down.

ANNIE

Maybe things'll be different in the West.

LIZZIE

Sure hope so.

EMMA

Hush! There is so much for you to tell us, my dear. Ah – my husband!

JOSIAH WEEKS enters, elegantly-dressed.

EMMA

Josiah, here's young Mrs Carlton, back from her honeymoon in the west.

MRS CARLTON

Not the true west, Mr Weeks – not as far as you'll be travelling – but we did see Texas, and it was a mighty fine sight.

JOSIAH

Welcome home. We shall be glad of any information you can afford us, Mrs Carlton.

His wife serves him tea.

JOSIAH

Thank you, Emma

LIZZIE

They picnicked all the time!

ANNIE

And she and Mr Carlton slept in the hay!

LIZZIE

Mrs Carlton says we should take a cow, for fresh milk!

MRS CARLTON

We did indeed miss the benefit of fresh eggs and milk, Mr Weeks, but George, my husband's old army sergeant, was most industrious in foraging for us and I can truly say there was not a day we did not dine in style.

JOSIAH

You were not too much out of comfort?

MRS CARLTON

Naturally, we had to rough it at times.

JOSIAH

Of course. We intend to cross a continent, Mrs Carlton!

EMMA offers MRS CARLTON the cake tray.

MRS CARLTON

Thank you. If it's not too brash to ask, why quit this pleasant spot?

JOSIAH

Land, Mrs Carlton, land. As much acreage as a man can see, in all directions – more, if he chooses and has the wherewithal.

ACT ONE

EMMA

It's all took up here. There's none to spare. *(Turns to her husband.)* Josiah, I don't know how the bank will get along without you.

JOSIAH

A man must expand his talents or fear the Lord.

EMMA

I won't deny it grieves me to think of leaving all our dear friends and neighbours. Weeks, even months, for a letter to reach us ...

ANNIE

We'll be back on visits, Ma. There'll be a railroad by then!

JOSIAH

Well, my decision is made, so there's an end to it. We go west. Lizzie, fetch pen and paper. You may write down any hints and notions our young friend is disposed to furnish us with.

EMMA

I only pray the weather's not inclement. Mr Weeks is liable to the rheumatics.

JOSIAH

We shall not travel in discomfort, Emma. A little roughing it will do none of us any harm, as you may see from our charming guest. No, this is a man's country. A challenge to true grit. Ahem. I would not say no to another muffin, if pressed, ladies.

The WOMEN swoop to his needs.

ACT ONE SCENE THREE

ASA MERCER, a well-dressed man, addresses us directly.

ASA MERCER

Young ladies ... young ladies! I come with an offer that I dare to think you will not lightly refuse. I need but a few more examples of what I see before me: the flower of our Eastern womanhood. If you do not seek adventure of the most respectable nature, ladies ... If you do not seek good fortune and happiness at the end of the trail, why then, dear ladies, walk away this instant! But I must tell you that there are those who await your presence in the new territories with respectful admiration ... Nay, dare I say, with love in their hearts. I speak of the brave boys who are seeking their fortunes in the silver mines of Nevada; in the rich golden soil of California. The men of the West await the soft bright radiance of your presence, asking only to cherish you with all the love and protection of true American pep. The future beckons! Don't hesitate! Positions with excellent wages await you – though any young woman who becomes immediately engaged will not be prevented from embarking, at once, on her life's destiny ... the ship of matrimony! California, young ladies! California!

On the other side of the stage, CATHERINE BEECHER, a soberly dressed woman, steps onto a podium. She has a fervent belief in her message. Her manner is quiet and un-histrionic.

CATHERINE BEECHER

Young women. I have an important message to convey to you. You are needed to fulfil a noble function. I

ACT ONE

come to acquaint you with a purpose that you may feel the need to engage upon – for God, and for your country. I speak of the education of our children in the western territory. Every day out in the West, men are deserting their posts for the lure of more profitable pursuits. Who better than women to fill the gap? A whole generation of children is in danger of being deprived of mental and moral instruction. I urge you, ladies, abandon your lives of shopping and dressing, calling and gossiping. Demand to offer a higher contribution. Go west, where you are needed! I believe it is we women who have the nature to be content with modest gain – who seek no gold mine but the shining eyes of our pupils. I must tell you: the going will not be easy. I know the life to be demanding and full of risk. But I say to you all – go west! Go west where our children are crying out for your devotion and your example. I implore you to answer the challenge. Go west, young woman!

ACT ONE SCENE FOUR

A STOREMAN, list in hand, and a poorly dressed YOUNG COUPLE. She is pregnant.

> STOREMAN
>
> Six sacks of corn, two sides of bacon ... green coffee beans, yeast, soda ...
>
> OLAF
>
> Erika?

ERIKA

A little faint . . . it's nothing.

STOREMAN

Lady feeling the heat?

ERIKA

Tell him I am well.

OLAF

She is well.

STORMAN

Pretty hard journey to be taking in that condition.

ERIKA

Finish the business. I shall be well.

OLAF

She is willing.

STOREMAN

Willing's one thing, doing's another. Danged if I'd take a wife of mine like that.

OLAF

We have no choice.

STOREMAN

Guess you know your own minds.

OLAF

I have to enquire about a handcart.

STOREMAN

A handcart? *(Laughs)* You don't mean for to say you intend to cross the states of America on foot?

ACT ONE

OLAF

(Serious)

We don't have the means for a wagon.

STOREMAN

You mean it, son? I guess you do. Here, a little gift for the lady. Hope it's a boy.

ACT ONE SCENE FIVE

LIZZIE and ANNIE are giggling over a book.

LIZZIE

(Reading) "They were the best-looking Indians I ever saw ... tall, strongly made, and light in colour. The glare of the fire fell on their bare, brawny arms and naked bodies." Naked bodies!

They giggle. Their mother, EMMA, enters with the DRESSMAKER. They hide the book.

EMMA

Here's Miss Amy, girls, to fit your outfits. Annie, since you intend to ride, we may as well see what kind of figure you intend to cut.

The DRESSMAKER fits ANNIE.

EMMA

Mr Weeks won't have the girls get into fast ways, that's for sure. How are the bonnets?

AMY

Just finishing the calico trim; real pretty colours.

EMMA

Calico?

LIZZIE

It's what they all wear, Ma. I read it in the journal.

AMY

I've put in plenty of tucks and a little fancy lace.

EMMA

(Looking in AMY's open bag.) Well, no sense in travelling without decent togs.

AMY

Oh, those are the latest merino shawls. You'll be needing them to keep out the cool of the evening.

EMMA

What do you think, girls?

ACT ONE SCENE SIX

FOUR IMMIGRANT WOMEN, poorly dressed, with bundles.

OVERSEER

Next. Next!

IMMIGRANT GIRL

He doesn't have to treat us like animals.

A well-dressed WOMAN – MRS BLAKE – approaches with an AGENT.

MRS BLAKE

My son-in-law's with the first cavalry. No sooner do they get a maid than she takes off and marries a soldier!

ACT ONE

AGENT

Here you are, Ma'am. Take your pick.

MRS BLAKE

The last one stayed barely three weeks!

MAN

Well, Ma'am, you won't see a homelier bunch than these females. Straight off the boat.

MRS BLAKE

Poor souls. They look miserable enough. Are they all bound for the west?

AGENT

That's right, Ma'am. Going for laundresses to the troops, that kind of thing. Great shortage of female labour.

MRS BLAKE

Maybe the little one at the end. She looks a clean body and goodness knows, no man could ever take a shine to her, if you'll pardon the expression.

AGENT

Just leave the arrangements to us, Mrs Blake.

MRS BLAKE

See that she's fixed up with a decent uniform. My husband will attend to the account for it.

OVERSEER

Right ... move out! I haven't got all day to attend to immigrant riffraff. Step on ... step on!

ACT ONE SCENE SEVEN

On the train.

Benches athwart to denote a train.

The passengers include MRS CARMODY and her young daughter MANDA, a UNION SOLDIER, MISS DORA, and a painted lady, LOLA, and her maid, PIECES.

MANDA
Look, Ma! Buffalo!

UNION SOLDIER
Them ain't buffalo young lady ... them's oxen.

MRS CARMODY
Manda, quit shoving ... Mighty big animals, soldier.

MISS DORA
I believe they haul the wagons.

UNION SOLDIER
Best thing out. What's more, you can feed off 'em when the going gits tough.

MISS DORA
If it's all the same to you, I'll stick to ham and eggs.

UNION SOLDIER
You'll be lucky to find that on the Plains, Ma'am.

MISS DORA
Won't we be stopping off for refreshments?

UNION SOLDIER
No sir. There ain't that kind of establishment. Not on the Plains.

ACT ONE

MISS DORA

But what is there, then?

UNION SOLDIER

Why nothing. Not a damn thing.

This produces a silence.

MRS CARMODY

I've heard there's wolves.

UNION SOLDIER

Yes, Ma'am, but don't fret yourself about that. A good wagon train will take care of you.

MANDA

Old Blue'll see them off. Paw's got a mighty fine dog ... Old Blue'll see them right off!

MRS CARMODY

She's crazy for that dog.

MANDA

Look, Ma – a cross!

UNION SOLDIER

See plenty of those on the trail. Except in Indian country. Cain't leave no crosses for some danged Indian to come grubbing up the corpse ... begging your pardon, Ma'am. But she'll see it soon enough.

MISS DORA

I was reading in the journal the Indians have been pretty badly done. Turned out of their villages and such.

SOLDIER

Don't you believe that, Miss – you ain't seen what I seen.

MISS DORA

Oh?

SOLDIER

Muh best friend was mutilated. I seen a good man fall with a arrow in his eye.

MOTHER

Oh hush!

SOLDIER

I ain't saying no more, Ma'am. Only they're fiends to me.

MISS DORA

Well, I'm sure we'll feel safe with you army boys around.

SOLDIER

Sure thing, miss! Yup. Only good injun's a dead injun.

VOICE

St. Louis! St Louis! End of the line!

Light change.

ACT ONE SCENE EIGHT

St. Louis.

The PASSENGERS alight on the platform. A COVERED WAGON is in evidence.

The TRAILMASTER and the WEEKS FAMILY enter severally.

PIECES

(To TRAILMASTER)

She say: is this here the wagon train?

ACT ONE

TRAILMASTER

Sure is, Topsy.

He moves away.

LOLA

Are we all right, Pieces?

PIECES

So he say.

LOLA

You better hop along then, and fix us a billet. Buck up ... What's the matter?

PIECES

I don't wanna go. I'm missing Sagaboy!

LOLA

Plenty of fellers where we're going. Fetch us a sarsaparilla, and buy one for yourself.

EMMA, LIZZIE and ANNIE approach.

EMMA

If I sit down to one more meal of beef and potatoes I shall throw up.

ANNIE

Hush, Ma. At least we have a bed in the hotel.

EMMA

Hotel, do you call it? All sleeping together like a passel of roosters, with the wind whistling through the walls. Your father will be ruined, the prices they have the neck to charge. We should quit right now.

LIZZIE

We must get used to roughing it, Ma.

ANNIE

Oh look, Lizzie – an Indian!

An INDIAN, with a brimmed black hat, and swathed in a blanket, draws close.

OLAF and ERIKA approach, looking bewildered. Manda's mother, MRS CARMODY, enters and exits.

MRS CARMODY

Have you seen a little girl?

PIECES returns with a drink.

LOLA

Where you been?

PIECES

Ain't no sarsaparilla. Had to settle for a root beer.

LOLA

Oh!

ANNIE

(*Looking at the INDIAN*) He looks quite human – apart from being swart in the face.

EMMA

Don't get too close, girls.

TRAILMASTER

(*To OLAF and ERIKA*)

You folks on the trail?

They confer.

LIZZIE

Imagine wearing a blanket in this heat!

ACT ONE

EMMA

I wonder how he came by that? That's a white man's blanket. Don't get too close. I warrant he's alive with bugs.

Enter a SNAKE-OIL SALESMAN.

EMMA jumps as he begins his spiel.

SNAKE-OIL SALESMAN

Ladies and gentlemen ... now, which of you fellers, which lady on behalf of a beloved child, has not spent money with the medical profession only to find persisting that same ailment what took 'em hurrying along in the first place? Ladies and gentlemen ... Folks ... Known tragedy muhself ... Lost muh first dear spouse, two little ones laid out right beside her. But I was blessed folks ... I was blessed. Travelled west to assuage muh grief, got pitched off muh horse, lay two days in a gulley, praying blue murder, with the buzzards overhead a-cawing for their supper. Raving with fever, folks, raving with fever, I was rescued by an Indian tribe of Exceeding Remoteness and carried to the teepee of their Chief ... Great Noble Face. You see me here before you today, fully recovered ... with muh dear present wife ... the Princess Chiwawa ... never a day of ill health, not even a female disorder. Friends, I am not a selfish man. Not for yours truly the uppity ways of the town medical man, a-hugging his lore to himself jest to squeeze another dollar from the weak widder, the ailing workin' man. No sirree! The secret cure I learned from those Indians I patented, as a remedy for folks who might meet with jest such a misfortune!

Friends ... do you suffer from the rheumatics, from the ague? From sore foot, pink eye, swollen thumb, the headache? Gumrot, toothache, bleeding, noises in the head? Dr Farnum's Elixir will see you through to perfect health! Unwillingly recognised by the medical profession for its efficaciousness in gripe, the distemper, nosebleeds, coughing in horses, for children's ailments: spots, boils, pimples – for its fast qualities in dyeing cloth – ladies and gentlemen, put ill health aside. The cure is in your pockets! And what do I ask for this precious, this irreplaceable elixir? Do I ask ten dollars a bottle? It's worth it! Do I ask five, it's cheap at the price ... do I ask three ... two ... that's giving it away ... Why, a rich cotton man in the South gave me a hundred dollars a bottle after his little girl was cured right out of the swoons – no! To you folks ... remember, I owe it my life ... to you the price is – one dollar! Ladies and gentlemen, don't miss this golden opportunity. Muh dear wife will now step among you.

PRINCESS CHIWAWA appears with a tray of medicine bottles.

SNAKE-OIL SALESMAN

Be sure not to miss this chance. May be quite a while afore we step this way again; there's other folks to cure ... How about a bottle for the pretty lady?

PIECES

He want us to pay for that?

LOLA

Don't worry.

ACT ONE

ANNIE

Jus' think! This time tomorrow we shall be on the trail!

EMMA

And not a day too soon. At least on the wagon I shall be mistress of my own house again. I've baked many a picnic loaf for your father in his hunting days ... I'm no stranger to the extempore, as you'll see. It's being rooked I can't abide. Lizzie, go fetch me a bottle of the doctor's medicine. I feel one of my headaches coming on.

TRAILMASTER

Trail's mustering up, folks. Get to your wagons, we're pulling out. No waiting for stragglers. We'll be counting heads in the hour, so look sharp. There's blankets still for sale, and hay ... *(To LOLA)* This way, Ma'am, hope you like the open air.

LOLA

Depends on the company, don't it?

Enter JOSIAH WEEKS, flustered.

EMMA

There you are! Thought you were half way to Fort Worth!

JOSIAH

Annie, you must content yourself not to horseback. There ain't an animal to be had! And to judge by the way women ride out here, no question of your aping that kind of caper.

ANNIE

Oh Pa, after all our contrivance!

JOSIAH

No daughter of mine's going to wear britches!

LIZZIE

Pa, did you get my ribbons?

JOSIAH

Ribbons!

EMMA

Who's going to shift the gear for us?

TRAILMASTER

Move yourselves. I ain't got all day!

EMMA

We need help.

TRAILMASTER

You got it. These two ... *(He indicates OLAF and ERIKA)* will be travelling with you. Be useful with the chores.

EMMA

Oh, we couldn't do that. There's barely enough sleeping room as it is.

TRAILMASTER

Sorry. You ain't got no choice.

EMMA

Josiah, do we stand for that?

TRAILMASTER

Likely to be the least of your troubles. Get ready to roll!

ERIKA pauses at EMMA's glare. OLAF helps load the wagon. EMMA makes a fuss about her china. The wagon is loaded.

ACT ONE

> TRAILMASTER
>
> Chain up! Wagons roll!

ACT ONE SCENE NINE

The Plains.

The tall INDIAN chants to the Great Spirit.

> INDIAN
>
> Ohh ... Ahh ... Eeeeeeh ... Ohh ... Ahh ... Eeeeeeh ...
> Ohh ... Ahh ... Eeeeeeh ...

ACT ONE SCENE TEN

Bright white light. The TRAILMASTER rides alongside the wagon-train.

> TRAILMASTER
>
> Keep up there ... keep up.

> OLAF
>
> We can't go faster.

> TRAILMASTER
>
> No stragglers.

> MRS DOLAN
>
> *(Irish)*
>
> It's this blamed dust. It gets into everything. The food, the water, in your eyes, your mouth. You get to hate yourself.

OLAF

Any chance of fresh meat?

TRAILMASTER

Not until we hit the fork, day after tomorrow. Liable to see some buffalo then.

ERIKA

I could not eat.

OLAF

Don't worry. I'll fix you something along the line.

MRS DOLAN

We're running low on water.

FRANCES DOLAN

(Her daughter)

It's the baby.

TRAILMASTER

Use rags and throw them away, Ma'am.

MRS DOLAN

Ain't nothin' we can dispose of.

TRAILMASTER

Use your petticoats. There'll be no more water till we reach the hole. Now, move on, and less complaining.

MRS DE WITT

There's a cross over there. What does it say?

MR DE WITT

I can't read it.

MRS DOLAN

It just says: 'Woman.'

Pause.

ACT ONE

TRAILMASTER

Wagons .... halt!

The WOMEN go into the wagon, brush their hair, relax, tend to one another. MANDA, the girl, calls to her dog.

OLAF, the TRAILMASTER, and an older man named ROCKY, sing 'Rye Whiskey.'

MRS DOLAN

Still suffering from the flow, Mrs Carmody?

MRS CARMODY (MANDA's mother) looks up.

MRS CARMODY

Yeah. Tried just about everything. Clothes is just hanging off me.

MRS DOLAN

Yup. We're pretty parched up ourselves.

MRS DE WITT

It's the children I fear for.

MRS DOLAN

Muh daughter here's all cramped up with the diarrhoea. Boiled up some rice but it takes the water. Miss Dora here baked for us. Grateful fer that.

MISS DORA

It was no trouble.

OLAF is sitting apart with SAM, an old miner, the TRAILMASTER, JOSIAH WEEKS, and MR DE WITT

OLAF

I'm willing to try anything, Sam. Anything to get a stake for my family.

SAM

Railroading's hard. Damn hard.

MRS CARMODY

(Calls)

Manda! Manda! Come git your supper!

FRANCES DOLAN

It ain't but jerked beef, Ma.

MRS DOLAN

Hit'll do. Food is food.

MRS DE WITT

Amen to that.

MRS DOLAN

I mind me of the time we wuz in Kentucky. Oh, they was bad times. Children all a-crying fur somethin' to eat. Remember that, Frances?

FRANCES DOLAN

I do.

MRS DOLAN

Did somethin' I wanted fur once. Took a fifty-pound sugar sack and muh old forty-five special – bein' a midwife, I carried it fur muh protection – and went on down to the commissary with muh son, little Henry, as he was. Hit was a-hearing the mothers and children crying whut did it.

MRS CARMODY

Why, what happened?

MRS DOLAN

Said to the clerk: well, Mister Martin, I says, it may be hard times, but I can always find a little somethin'

to git by on. Gimme a 24-pound sack of flour. And I
whispers to muh little son Henry: take this here sack
o' flour and walk out. Which he done. Then I called
fur the things as was most necessary, filled up my
sugar sack, and then I sez, now Martin, I sez, I'll see
you in ninety days, soon as ever I kin git the money,
I sez. I have some starvin' children to feed and they
won't wait. He sez: Aunt Molly, he sez, don't you walk
outta this store without payin' fur those groceries. I
pulled out the pistol and I sez: Martin, if you tries to
take this grub I'll shoot you, if they's to hang me for
it tomorrow mornin'. And I walked out. And, by God,
those children was so hungry that when the mother
was a-makin' up the dough, they was grabbing it
off her hands and cramming it into their mouths.
Course, by the time I got back to my own door, the
sheriff was there to arrest me.

MANDA

Did you go to jail, Mrs Dolan?

MRS DOLAN

Nope. He sez to me, he sez: Aunt Molly, what in the
world! Have you turned out for to be a robber? I sez,
oh no, Frank, I'm no robber, but I've heard these little
children cry out till I'm desperate and nearly out of
my mind. I'll get out and collect the money just as
soon as I am able. You know I'm honest as the day is
long. And the tears come in his eyes and he sez: Aunt
Molly, he sez, I come up here to arrest you, but if
you ... if you got the heart to do that for other people's
children, he sez, I'll pay that bill myself. And he sez,
if they fire me for not arresting you, why then I'll be
glad of it. And he walked out, and he didn't arrest me.

SAM

Best money on the railroad is working on ahead, with the surveying party. They'll take a laborer or two, if he's an agile man. Git picked off by Indians though.

OLAF

I just need to get started.

SAM

Work as a blaster, or a bridge monkey; that's good pay. Then there's the graders. Breaking down the rock, laying the track ... pretty heavy labour. Timbers is all cut and sawn ahead and sent back, d'yuh see? Maybe rust-eating's the best job. Yup. Working in teams of four; whipping the rails off the truck, spike, couple, and bolt. *(Makes the sound of tightening a nut.)* By golly, some of those teams lay four rails a minute; pile up the pelf that way.

OLAF

How come you quit?

SAM

Silver mines.

OLAF

Silver mines? Is there a real chance of a strike?

SAM

I wouldn't recommend it to ya. Not for a man with a family.

FRANCES DOLAN

Coffee!

OLAF, SAM, the TRAILMASTER, JOSIAH and MR DE WITT join the women.

ACT ONE

MRS DOLAN

Sure feels a whole lot better with victuals inside you.

MRS DE WITT

I never thought to be using buffalo droppings for firewood.

TRAILMASTER

Never fear, Ma'am. Improves the taste!

Laughter.

MISS DORA

Just think ... in California, there'll be fruit for the picking right outside your door.

MRS DE WITT

I read of a woman looking up from her wash-basket; sees a vein of silver in the rock, wide as a side of beef.

EMMA, and her daughters, LIZZIE and ANNIE, enter.

OLAF

They say the gold lies in nuggets at your feet.

EMMA

It certainly puts a shine on the whole endeavour.

MRS CARMODY

Everyone walking about in silk and fine hats, all free and equal.

MANDA

And rich, Ma, and rich!

MRS DOLAN
(Smiling)

Hush, child.

MANDA

We'll be rich!

MUSIC. Light change to low.

ANNIE stands apart, looking at the stars. The TRAILMASTER joins her.

ANNIE

So peaceful.

He does not answer. She looks at him.

ANNIE

I guess we can't complain.

TRAILMASTER

Nope.

ANNIE

The journey has been hard, I don't deny.

TRAILMASTER

Hard? Ma'am, we ain't even started yet.

SOUND of Indian drums.

ACT ONE SCENE ELEVEN

ARMY GENERAL, the ARMY AGENT and a ceremonially dressed INDIAN CHIEF.

GENERAL

The great father in Washington wants you all to be his friends, and friends to the white man. If you agree to our terms, he wishes to make presents to you and to your people as a token of his friendship.

ACT ONE

AGENT

The general, you must understand, is not here to ask you to make peace, but to advise you that you may have it by signing the treaty.

The CHIEF does not reply.

GENERAL

Chief, you may as well know it. The white man is coming out here so fast that nothing can stop it.

AGENT

The general is right. It will be like a prairie fire in a high wind. Nothing can stop it, nothing.

GENERAL

The whites are a numerous people. They require room and cannot help but take it.

AGENT

We realise it is hard for you to leave your land, and the graves of your ancestors but, unfortunately, these men are now in your country and there is no portion where you may live but you will come in contact with them. The consequence is that you are in constant danger of being imposed upon, and you have to resort to arms in self-defence. Under the circumstances, you must see that it is in the best interests of your people.

CHIEF

Look at me. I am a part of this land where the sun rises. Now you wish us to go where the sun sets. The great father says that he is kind to us. I do not think so. When he sent us soldiers and agents who told us to behave well, we did so. We welcomed the white man.

AGENT

Chief White Cloud, there is no reason why your people should not be the most happy and prosperous Indians in the whole United States. *(Aside, to General)* Believe me, General, t'will be cheaper to feed these people than to fight them. *(To the Chief)* You must give the General answer.

CHIEF

I have no pockets wherein to put your talk. Words do not pay for my country, nor give my people a home where they can live. *(Pause)* A river will run backwards before any man born free will be content to be denied liberty to go where he pleases. Let us be free men. Free to think and talk and act for ourselves. Leave us our freedom and we will follow your advice.

GENERAL

I can't listen to this.

AGENT

You must consider your options, Chief. I have explained everything to you.

CHIEF

We will not leave our country.

GENERAL

Call an end to the parley.

AGENT

General Carlton ...

GENERAL

There will be no further council with the Indians. No more talk. Lock him up.

ACT ONE

AGENT
The Chief was offered safe conduct.

CHIEF
Your women are here. We will not spill blood in this place. *(He stands.)* If you wish to send your soldiers after us, let us get a little distance, and there let us make bloody the ground.

GENERAL
You have till tomorrow morning. After that, my soldiers will hunt you down. No peace on any terms! This war shall be pursued against you until you cease to exist. *(To AGENT)* Take your savage away.

Light change.

ACT ONE SCENE TWELVE

MRS DOLAN furiously kneads a bowl of washing.

MRS DOLAN
I don't make the sense of it, I really don't. I never heard of an illness taking off so many people, not all at once. There's no sickness can take a whole family that way, all in the space of three days. How are we to eat all that fodder, the old woman and me? It's too much for two women to eat and, my God, there's the cart. How are we to manage that and all the gear? That's not a woman's work. Perhaps t'was the lack of water. Well, that's off me mind now. He's at rest, and I wish I were too, with the old man. God knows how we'll get on. It'll be the laundering again, arms cracked up with soda, the way it was before. I've seen

it all. Didn't I lose three before birth and two after?
Not to mention the little girl, sitting up with her
three days and nights and her just laying there and
dying on me, and the priest telling me it was the good
Lord loved her so, and the old mother crying into her
shawl, not a bit of use – and not a piece of bread in the
house, and every spud rotten. Oh, there's a lot owing,
I'm telling you. There's plenty owing. And where's it
to come from? Who's going to pay for it?

ACT ONE SCENE THIRTEEN

The TRAVELLERS on the wagon-train enter severally. The
WOMEN are wearing clean bonnets for the Sabbath. They kneel
and pray at random. The PREACHER walks among the kneeling,
praying flock.

MRS CARMODY
Will you take a prayer, sister?

MRS DE WITT
With your blessing, sister. Dear Lord, you have seen
fit to bring us to the test with sickness and sorrow.

The others respond, praising the Lord in an undertone, calling out
His name, or repeating the end of the speaker's sentences.

MRS DE WITT
We know you love us, Lord, and that you wish us to
abide in Thee. Give us Thy strength and protection
through this baleful land. Give us the strength of
Samson, the wisdom of Elijah ... Protect us, O Lord.

ACT ONE

VOICES

Protect us ... worship Thy name ... lead us into Righteousness ... hallowed be His name ...

PREACHER

It bein' the Lord's day, this trail comes to a restful halt while we gathers to give praise to God fur His mercy and goodness, and to worship His name!

VOICES

Worship His name ... praise the Lord!

PREACHER

Likewise, to ask His blessing on all us souls gathered together – and one or two faces as I notice is missing.

VOICE #1

God strike the Unbeliever!

VOICE #2

Praise His name!

PREACHER

Likewise, to ask divine support and protection on this long and arduous journey to whut we fully believe is gonna be the Promised Land!

VOICES

Hallelujah! Praise the Lord! Praise His name! Hallelujah!

PREACHER

There's people among us of different denominations, Lord. Some of us come from way off in foreign parts. Cain't even understand a word of God's English. They come to us from heathen places where they wasn't even allowed to hallow Thy name in a quiet and sociable way without frills and the worship of idols.

Please God, we all intend to reach territory where we can spread the word of the Lord to one and all; to painted savages, in a manner that's decent and in words for to be heard and understood by the whole congregation, and not just some!

VOICES
Hallelujah! Praise Jesus! Praise His name!

PREACHER
Folks, we have all of us here – just taken off!

VOICES
Taken off!

PREACHER
We have responded to the call of Manifest Destiny!

VOICES
Manifest Destiny!

PREACHER
I call on all you sinners to cleanse your hearts and souls for the test!

VOICES
For the test! Hallelujah!

PREACHER
Give yourselves to Jesus!

VOICES
I do! ... I do!

PREACHER
Come to the Lord!

VOICES
I come ... I come!

ACT ONE

PREACHER

Come to Jesus!

VOICES

I'm a-coming ... I'm coming, Lord!

PREACHER

Let me hear it now ... Let me hear you coming!

VOICES

Oh Lord! Take me, Lord! I'm coming, Jesus! I'm coming, Lord!

PREACHER

Come to the Lord! Come to His bosom! Let me hear you now! Come to Jesus! Will somebody catch that female over there before she keels over. Praise them Lord!

The congregation breaks into an ecstatic hymn, moving in rhythm.

ACT ONE SCENE FOURTEEN

The TRAVELLERS move across the stage slowly. EMMA stops, and is passed by others. Her FAMILY stop.

EMMA

It's no use, Josiah. I can't go on.

She sits down mutinously, her arms around her knees.

JOSIAH

Come on, old girl.

EMMA

I'm not your old girl. Shut up, I say. Shut up!

ANNIE

Come on, Ma. We'll get you a ride later on.

LIZZIE

The sick have to be cared for. They can't walk.

EMMA

It's our wagon! We should ride. That man's a crook.

ANNIE

No, he ain't, Ma. If you were sick you'd be in the wagon. Think of it that way.

JOSIAH

Get up, Emma. There's folk passing us. We mustn't straggle. It's dangerous.

EMMA

Dangerous! There's nothing here but nothing!

JOSIAH

Emma, you know that everything that breathes here bites. Everything that grows stings. Get up.

EMMA

No. I've a mind to stay where I am.

Sighing, he gives her the water bottle. She grabs it greedily, spilling the precious liquid. He wrestles it back.

JOSIAH

Now hold on! You girls get ahead. Your Ma and I will follow.

The GIRLS go off. OLAF passes with his WIFE.

OLAF

Better get along there, friend. Trail boss is right behind.

ACT ONE

JOSIAH

Thanks, we'll be along. You hear that, Emma? Emma, now listen here. I'm not disposed to take any more of your nonsense. I've suffered the wrong side of your tongue since we hit the fort. You should be grateful to God we weren't took by the cholera. Deuce knows how we came out of it alive, but we did. And I don't intend to let you give way into mindlessness. So, if you don't get up on your feet, I'm going to shake you up, which is a thing I never expected to have to do. Now, do you hear me?

EMMA

I ain't moving, and that's that.

He tries to lift her up. She spits in his face.

JOSIAH

Emma! Now I know you're not yourself! *(Tries to haul her to her feet.)* Come on. Get up!

EMMA

Look at you! What do you think you look like? Your nose is all burnt up, your cheeks blistered with alkali; you look like a critter from hell. You ain't Josiah Weeks. I don't know you. My husband wouldn't drag me across this baking oven. I'm a respectable woman! You promised me! You promised me we'd travel in comfort, like civilised folk. You lied to me. You're a liar! You're a liar! Well, I ain't moving and you can suit yourself.

JOSIAH

There's no-one behind us but the trailmaster. We'll see what he has to say.

                    EMMA

I ain't moving.

                    JOSIAH

If you don't get up this instant, I shall walk off and leave you. *(She does not move.)* I mean it, wife. Very well, if that's the way you want it.

He goes. The TRAILMASTER enters.

                    TRAILMASTER

What's this?

                    EMMA

I ain't moving.

The TRAILMASTER screws up his eyes and looks off.

                    TRAILMASTER
                    (Calls)

Weeks! Weeks, is that you? Come and git your wife!

                    JOSIAH
                    (Approaches)

She won't budge. I'm trying to trick her on.

                    TRAILMASTER

Well, it ain't worked. See to it, man.

                    JOSIAH

Mr Ames, I'm out of notions. She won't get up.

                    TRAILMASTER

She's your wife. You can't leave her here. Take your strap to her, man. There's no other way. I've seen it before – man and beast.

JOSIAH takes off his belt and flails at his WIFE – shouting to give himself the nerve to do it.

ACT ONE

JOSIAH

Get up! Get up, you cat! Get up, you varmint!

Holding her arms over her head, to shield herself from the blows, EMMA staggers to her feet and runs off.

ACT ONE SCENE FIFTEEN

The Desert.

The TRAILMASTER comes on with a WIZENED OLD-TIMER of odd appearance. Apart, the WOMEN walk on severally, and gaze out at the desert.

OLD-TIMER

Now, hold on. You hold on, son. Jest hold on. Hit ain't that easy. Question of know-how.

TRAILMASTER

Make your deal.

They confer.

MISS DORA

Nothing but salt wastes. It seems like the hand of death is upon us.

MRS DOLAN

The animals is dropping. Ain't but barely a team of oxen left. We shoulda hit water by now.

OLD -TIMER

Willing to pay, are yuh? Willing to pay? Ye don't have the wherewithal.

TRAILMASTER

I'm willing to offer a fair price.

Apart, MRS DE WITT prays on her knees.

MRS CARMODY

(Nodding towards the praying woman)
She had a miserable day yesterday. Her husband died.

MRS DE WITT

Oh God, look down and grant us Thy favour not to let us perish in this cruel and hateful wilderness.

MRS CARMODY

Reckon He's looking in the other direction.

OLD-TIMER

Bunch of critters you seen fit to bring in here, messing up the territory, gonna need more know-how than you got the wit to provide.

TRAILMASTER

State your terms, man!

OLD-TIMER

Go on, strike me down. See where it will git you!

TRAILMASTER

Are you gonna help us or ain't you?

They begin to move off.

OLD-TIMER

Folks should stay where they belongs. Desert belongs to them as is fit fer it. How many mules you got?

MISS DORA

It's funny. All those hours I spent embroidering holy texts. Sewing straight seams. Making fine handkerchiefs. It seems everything I ever learned was useless.

ACT ONE

MRS CARMODY

I know what you mean.

MRS DOLAN

We're losing our shape.

MRS DE WITT

Lord take pity on us. Show us the way.

EMMA enters, and gazes out at the horizon with them.

EMMA

We are nowhere. Nowhere at all.

ACT ONE SCENE SIXTEEN

A rough interior. One wall is plastered with pink sheets from the Police Gazette. The furniture is primitive. ANNIE and LIZZIE are washing in a tin bath.

LIZZIE

I surely wish I'd stayed back at Fort Riley with Maretta.

ANNIE

She was taking an awful chance. A soldier's pay ain't that good.

LIZZIE

I figured that. Still, to be married to a man in blue. Maretta's feller looked a mighty fine sight.

ANNIE

What if he gets killed?

LIZZIE

She could marry another one! *(They giggle.)* Say, you know what I just saw? The painted lady playing poker with the men. They say she's winning a passel of money on the trail.

ANNIE

Hey, did you notice the walls? It's the Police Gazette. Ma says not to look, it's too racy. Take a read. I'll watch the door.

LIZZIE reads.

ANNIE

I'm sure yearning to get to Fort Laramie.

LIZZIE

(Reads)

Yeah.

ANNIE

Not that I'm not grateful to spell up in this place. Makes you real happy to be setting under a roof again, even if it's made of mud.

LIZZIE

(Reading the wall)

Uhuh. Wow!

ANNIE

Wild stories, huh?

LIZZIE

(Crouching)

Wonder who lived here?

ANNIE

Whoever it was had to walk a mile to that miserable little crick.

ACT ONE

LIZZIE

Maybe they had a mule.

ANNIE doesn't reply. An INDIAN (WATANYE) has walked in the door. He is part-naked, and painted. ANNIE stands, her mouth open.

LIZZIE

I said, maybe they had a mule ...

LIZZIE sees the INDIAN and screams.

The INDIAN advances on ANNIE and inspects her. He is fascinated by her yellow hair. He advances. She shoos him with her apron.

ANNIE

Shoo! Shoo!

He steps back, puzzled. He dips his fingers into the pot of soap and tastes it.

ANNIE

Hey! That's soap!

Challenged, he eats some more proudly, eyes blinking.

He advances on ANNIE again. She stands her ground. He takes out his knife. LIZZIE trembles violently.

He lifts a lock of ANNIE's hair. Once she realizes he's not going to scalp her, she rallies. She picks up a pair of scissors and cuts a piece of her hair for him. He slices off a lock of his hair with his knife, gives it to her, and goes.

The GIRLS stare at each other, transfixed.

END OF ACT ONE

ACT TWO

ACT TWO SCENE ONE

A simple room.

A STENOGRAPHER. The COLONEL enters, sits at table. ANNIE enters with the COLONEL'S WIFE. The COLONEL rises.

COLONEL
Would you care to take a seat, Miss Weeks?

ANNIE
If it's all the same, Colonel, I'd prefer to stand.

COLONEL
As you wish. This, of course, is an official investigation. It is not to be published in the newspapers, or anything of that kind. I wish to hear the whole truth in regard to the matter. Just consider yourself on the witness stand. If the Ute Indians are guilty, the government will punish them, and we must know the truth.

ANNIE
I understand, sir.

COLONEL
Will you place your hand on the Bible and repeat after me ... I swear to tell the truth, the whole truth, and nothing but the truth. So help you God.

She puts her hand on the Bible.

ACT TWO

ANNIE

I swear to tell the truth, the whole truth, and nothing but the truth. So help me God.

COLONEL

Wouldn't you rather sit down, Miss Weeks?

ANNIE

No sir. I'd rather stand. I feel more comfortable.

COLONEL

Very well. *(He clears his throat.)* How long did ... *(He refers to his notes for the name.)* How long did Watanye keep you with him?

ANNIE

All the time.

COLONEL

He had you all the time.

ANNIE

Yes sir.

COLONEL

Was he willing at any time to let you go?

ANNIE

I asked him repeatedly. He couldn't seem to make up his mind.

COLONEL

Were you well treated?

ANNIE

(After a pause.) No better than what I expected. I had heard of their natures on the trail.

COLONEL

Miss Weeks, we have to have the whole truth.

ANNIE

I understand that, sir. We were all insulted a good many times, including my mother. We expected to be.

COLONEL

What do you mean by insult, and of what did it consist?

ANNIE

Of outrageous treatment at night.

COLONEL

Am I to understand that they outraged you several times during the nights that you were with them?

ANNIE

Yes sir.

COLONEL

They forced you against your will?

ANNIE

Yes sir.

COLONEL

Did they threaten to kill you if you did not comply?

ANNIE

Oh no. Only on the one occasion. I asked him if he wanted to kill me. He said 'Yes.' I said 'Get up and shoot me then, and leave me alone.' He turned over and didn't do anything more that night.

COLONEL

Was it a constant thing?

ACT TWO

ANNIE

Yes sir.

COLONEL

How long after the actual capture did the outrages take place.

ANNIE

They began the same night. The Monday. A good many times I pushed him off, made a fuss, and raised a difficulty.

COLONEL

Was it done while his own squaws were in the tent?

ANNIE

Yes sir. Sometimes on the ground outside.

COLONEL

And they knew about it?

ANNIE

Yes sir. Watanye's squaw said I must not make a fuss about it. I think she felt sorry for me. But she didn't dare do anything.

COLONEL

Did any of the other men do the same thing to you?

ANNIE

Oh, no sir. He took me as his squaw and the rest dared not come near.

COLONEL

None of the others came near you?

ANNIE

No sir.

COLONEL

Did he say anything when he released you?

ANNIE

The day you came?

COLONEL

Yes.

ANNIE

He asked me, the day before, what I was going to tell... He said: 'You say the Utes are no good.' I said I wouldn't. He... he asked me to stay in the camp and be his squaw. He said I should not have to work like the other women if I would stay with him. I said no, I couldn't do that. He seemed very upset. I... I've heard he's behaving oddly in the compound.

COLONEL

You need not concern yourself on that score, Miss Weeks. He did not seem to think it was wrong?

ANNIE

Oh no, sir. They think it a pretty good thing to have a white squaw, a white woman.

COLONEL

Did you see any clothes in anyone's possession?

ANNIE

One Indian had father's shoes on. They were all pretty drunk, and throwing goods around.

COLONEL

Did you see Mr McBride's coat?

ANNIE

No sir.

ACT TWO

COLONEL

Did you hear anyone say who killed Mr Whaley and Mr McBride?

ANNIE

No sir. My father says he would recognise the Indian who struck down Mr Brough.

COLONEL

I see. Thank you, Miss Weeks. Have you told this to anybody besides yer mother?

ANNIE

No sir.

COLONEL

And no-one else shall know. We are grateful for your testimony.

The COLONEL'S WIFE rises.

ANNIE

Sir, what will happen to Watanye?

COLONEL

They will all be tried and punished according to the law.

ANNIE

I ... I just wanted to say that, on the whole, he ... he looked after me pretty well, according to his style ... and I believe he is the cause of my father being alive. I ... I requested it of him.

The COLONEL looks up at her keenly. He knows what she means.

COLONEL'S WIFE

Come, my dear. We must leave the army to decide the case.

During the above scene, WATANYE, apart, daubs himself with black, watched by his SQUAW. As ANNIE leaves the courtroom, he howls in anguish.

> ANNIE
>
> *(Jumps nervously)*
>
> What is that noise?
>
> COLONEL'S WIFE
>
> Oh, that's just an Indian.
>
> ANNIE
>
> It sounds as though he's in torture!
>
> COLONEL'S WIFE
>
> No, no ... they hate to be confined. Don't worry your head, my dear. They don't feel things as we do.
>
> ANNIE
>
> Of course not.

WATANYE howls again as the WOMEN go.

Light change.

ACT TWO SCENE TWO

Two young Indian war chiefs.

> RED EAGLE
>
> Our hearts are sore for you. Many of our blood are among your dead.
>
> DULL KNIFE
>
> We sought no war. The treaty promises were broken. To stay meant to die. We thought it better to die fighting, so we came here.

ACT TWO

RED EAGLE

You are welcome to share our lands. In the Spring we will make war. The Sioux and the Cheyenne are blood brothers. We will descend like a swarm of bees.

DULL KNIFE

The Cheyenne have made mistakes. When we fought the soldiers and they ran away, we did not pursue them and kill them. We showed we were the bravest and we thought that was enough. We did not understand that they meant to kill us all.

RED EAGLE

The white man has taken our country. The white man has taken our game. The white man has taken our women. Now no peace. We will raise the battle axe until death.

ACT TWO SCENE THREE

A Saloon. MAC, the saloon-keeper, PIECES and LOLA, are drinking with VERA, the saloon owner.

VOICES

Look out, here comes Jim McCourt ... Get off the streets. It's McCourt!

MRS DE WITT rushes in, and then gapes as she realizes where she is. SHOTS offstage.

LOLA

What's up?

COWBOY

(Sticks his head in the door.)

It's Jim McCourt, Vera!

He goes.

VERA

I figured. *(Stops MRS DE WITT from leaving.)* I wouldn't.

PIECES

This ain't the mission hall!

VERA

Best be safe. He won't come in here.

LOLA

Why not?

VERA

Owes me money. Set down a spell, Ma'am. Mac, give the lady a drink.

MRS DE WITT

Thank you, but I never touch liquor.

VERA

Suit yourself. Set down. *(MRS DE WITT, troubled, sits. VERA turns to LOLA.)* You could do worse than take a piece of this place. I do good business.

LOLA

Thanks, but we're headed for 'Frisco.

VERA

Think about it. *(To MRS DE WITT)* On the trail, huh?

More GUNSHOTS. MRS DE WITT jumps. The others ignore it.

ACT TWO

LOLA

(To VERA)

No, like I was saying, the mining camp was no place to make a living. Mud! We set up in a pup tent, remember Pieces? Wind blowing down on top of us. That hurried the boys along!

PIECES

Business was great.

PIECES glares coldly at MRS DE WITT.

MRS DE WITT

(Finding her courage)

Miss Pieces, did you ... did you never think of giving your soul to Jesus?

PIECES

Jesus? Why, woman, what he ever do for me?

MRS DE WITT

We must have faith.

PIECES

Oh, I got that. Muh faith's in survivin', ain't that right, Mac?

MAC refills their glasses; gives MRS DE WITT coffee. VERA slips a little whisky into the cup, unseen by MRS DE WITT.

MRS DE WITT

But this ... this travail that we're suffering ... I believe it's God's purpose ...

MAC, the barman, inclines noncommittally.

MRS DE WITT

... and that this territory can give us all a fresh start. If I didn't believe that, why I don't think I could continue.

LOLA

Know what you mean.

MRS DE WITT

Forgive me for saying this, Miss Boolay, but you don't seem like a bad woman. You strike me as being very kind and understanding.

LOLA

(Preening)

I guess we've all seen trouble, Mrs de Witt. I know I have. You'd be surprised what we have to put up with.

PIECES

Why don't you just shut up?

LOLA

What? Oh, sorry. Didn't mean to offend. Only there wasn't much choice of situation when me and Pieces hit the Plains.

MRS DE WITT

But I gather you mean to change your way of life.

PIECES

Now, don't you be too sure about that. Plenty of Misses keen enough to make their pile on their backs. Ain't nuthin' wrong with pleasure.

LOLA

Why don't you lay off that bottle?

ACT TWO

PIECES

If a man's prepared to pay for it ... Don't she get payment? Board and lodgin' and a ring on her finger? Her sort ain't gonna give nuthin' away. Leastways, not till the bargain's struck.

MRS DE WITT

There is such a thing as hallowed conjugal love, Miss ...

PIECES

Fontanne. Di Fontanne. Miz di Fontanne.

MRS DE WITT

Believe me, Miss di Fontanne, I don't wish to make comment on your way of life. I've seen so much suffering on the trail that my mind is a good deal more open than when I was teaching music in Arroway Falls. Of course, there wasn't the temptation there.

PIECES

Oh, now you listen here, preacher lady. There's always temptation when you're a piece of goods that men thinks is available for their purpose. I've seen many a good girl picked off on the way home from chapel. Question of how you're favoured, ain't it?

VERA

Hold on, Pieces ...

PIECES

Maybe you plain women don't see too much of that aspect of things. Think yourself lucky some fool push a ring on your finger. Favour you with a couple of brats ...

MRS DE WITT

That is not true. That is just not true.

PIECES

And what would a woman looking like you know about it? Who's ever gonna take a second look in your direction?

LOLA

Pieces!

PIECES

Tellin' us to get back to Jesus! Why, woman, you ain't got no place else to go! I'm in a position to know how often your husband's likely to pleasure himself under his own roof.

MRS DE WITT

That is not true! My husband was an ... an active man. I spent my life worrying that we'd get another child. What do you know about it? You avoid all that. And I wish you would tell me how. Not that I ... It's a woman's destiny and privilege to bear children. I don't seek to avoid my joy. But I want a roof over my head, and it's not too much to ask! *(She drinks.)* A roof, and a piece of grass for the children to play on. And I guess I'd like to be fixed so that I could look at a book now and then.

VERA

A book?

MRS DE WITT

I have a terrible weakness for reading. There's little place for that in a woman's life. It makes me guilty when I steal time that way.

ACT TWO

VERA adds whisky to MRS DE WITT's cup. The door bursts open and JIM MCCOURT enters and shoves past PIECES.

                    JIM

Git your black ass outta my way.

He goes. NELL enters quickly. She is older, dressed in buckskin; carries a six-gun.

                    NELL

Whur'd he go?

PIECES lifts her eyes upwards.

                    NELL

By golly, Jim. Jim! Come down here now, ya hear me?
If you don't come down here this instant, I'm
a-coming up to git you!

                    VERA
                 (Sing-song)

He'll kill you!

                    MAC

She's right, Nell.

                    VERA

Shut up and have a drink.

                    NELL
               (Of Mrs de Witt)

Who the hell's that?

                    VERA

This lady's come in out of Jim's way.

                    NELL

Picked a good spot.

LOLA

We're looking after her.

NELL

(Takes a good look.)

I reckon you're safe enough, Ma'am. Yuh looks too pious for to be sweet-talked by Lady Black Cat there. Let's have a shot, Mac.

LOLA

Stage is in then?

NELL

Looks like it, don't it? By golly, muh hands is red hot. Muh lead horse went lame on me this side a Cherakee. New feller fair tore the guts outta hisself. Never should've picked a roan.

VERA

(To MRS DE WITT)

She's been out here twenty years. Here, you was married, wasn't you Nell?

NELL

More'n once. Muh last feller went over a cliff celebrating his birthday. Took his job meself. Needed the money.

MAC

Where you been, Nell?

NELL

Got meself in a mite of trouble over to Wyoming. *(Drinks, laughs.)* Damnedest thing you ever did see. Like I sez, gits meself in a little fracas over settlement of a bill. I'm taken up before the Bench ... God strike me dead if'n the jedge ain't a little old lady!

ACT TWO

PIECES

You're kidding!

NELL

Kiss a horse's ass if I'm lyin'. 'Ma'am,' I sez 'Ma'am, I'm just a poor defenceless woman like yourself... it was them three great hulking critters like whut you sees a-setting over there telling lies, agin yours truly, five foot three.' Made no danged bit of difference. Thirty days.

MAC

A woman judge?

NELL

Ain't no lie. Damnedest little old grandmother, setting up there on a cushion bawling louder'n a hogcaller. Sure makes you think.

PIECES

Maybe things is looking up.

NELL

Don't git ideas. It was still thirty days in the cooler.

LOLA

Yeah, reckon we'll be paying side money just the same. Still...

MRS DE WITT

(Getting talkative from the whisky)

Yes, why not? I've seen women on the trail do anything a man can do – endure any suffering.

NELL

Women gits the worst of it all right. See how them squaws is treated up in the hills. Met a young'un on the trail a week back. By golly, if she hadn't been wedded to a white man for seven years and he'd turned her out of doors for a yeller-haired Swede from Dakota.

MRS DE WITT

His own wife?

NELL

There was the ring, still on her finger. 'Bout all he'd left her with, bar the two pups. I threw her off a sack of flour and a twist of taffy for the little'uns. All I had to offer. How much is muh reckoning, Mac? Can't stand around with a bunch of women all day. I got a stage to take out. Good luck to ye.

She goes.

VERA

She'll die on the trail.

PIECES

With her boots on.

JIM bursts in. He passes PIECES. The WOMEN watch warily as he takes a drink.

JIM

Women!

He spits. As he approaches the exit, MRS DE WITT, who has risen in alarm, is in his way. She holds up her brolly for self-protection.

He knocks her out and goes.

LOLA

She's out cold. Mrs de Witt? Out cold.

PIECES

Foolish woman. *(Shrugs, draws on her cigar.)* Wrong timing.

ACT TWO

Sound of fracas. EMMA enters, boxing JIM's ears. He tries to kiss her. She clocks him, and throws him out. JOSIAH enters, amazed.

EMMA

He broke my eggs!

ACT TWO SCENE FOUR

Back on the trail.

The WOMEN and MEN are now very gaunt. Their hair is bleached, their clothes denuded of colour. MRS DOLAN takes some ragged clothes from a line strung from the wagon. She turns over the rags, shaking her head.

MRS DOLAN

Don't know why I took the trouble. Thought it might freshen 'em up a spell. Mighta knowed the wind would get to them. *(Lifts her head and sniffs.)* Mmm! Smells good! What is it?

MRS CARMODY

Apache scout picked me up a mother porcupine a-ways down the trail. Beat its head in for me. My, didn't the little ones howl for their Ma! But we took 'em anyway.

MRS DOLAN

Nothing like a piece of meat to give you strength. Since we ate the mules, there don't seem to be a living thing alive. Muh daughter's getting sore in the vitals ... there ain't but a few grits and tack inside us to stop our bones knocking together.

MRS CARMODY
There's an orphan kid down the line has a dog.
Not but it ain't pure skeleton. God knows how she
managed to keep it so long from getting ate up. You
could offer her fifty cents for it.

ERIKA enters, her BABY on her back.

ERIKA
I wondered where the smell was coming from.

MRS CARMODY
Sorry, I got mouths to feed.

ERIKA
I'd be happy to boil the bones for a little soup for the
baby.

MRS CARMODY
Sure wish I could oblige.

She turns away from ERIKA, who stands for a while, hoping.

Then she goes.

MRS CARMODY
She might as well content herself to losing that child.
It ain't never gonna see the winter.

MRS DOLAN
I could trade you a hand of citric crystals for the pelt.
I knows you don't have none.

They pore over the trade. MRS CARMODY hands over the pelt.

MRS CARMODY
There ain't too much of it.

MRS DOLAN
Better than naught. I mind me of the first deer Mr

ACT TWO

Jackson took, way back along the trail. My daughter's youngest was watching him skin it, and took to crying over the dead critter. She seen it twitching under the knife. 'Oh Daddy,' she says, 'the deer wants her dress back.' You couldn't help but smile. We ate pretty good then.

She goes. ERIKA returns.

ERIKA
I'd be willing to take the skin off you for a few phosphorous matches.

MRS CARMODY
I'm real sorry. She just took it. There's naught but a quill or two. You're welcome to seek.

ERIKA scrabbles on the ground for scraps.

ACT TWO SCENE FIVE

The TRAILMASTER and the INDIAN SCOUT are crouching, looking at the ground.

TRAILMASTER
What do you make of it?

INDIAN SCOUT
Pretty small trail. From moccasin print, Cheyenne – not Sioux.

TRAILMASTER
Good. Hunting party I'd guess. How long ago?

INDIAN SCOUT

Grass pretty damn dead. Two, three days. Horse dung done dry. Grass in dung say horses from Catchicou.

TRAILMASTER

They're likely to be headed back south then?

INDIAN SCOUT

(Sniffing around) Horse piddle back of prints here. That means mares. War party no ride mares. Hunting party for sure.

TRAILMASTER

Good. That's okay. I reckon we're clear for the big climb.

He looks up at the mountains.

INDIAN SCOUT

Snows come early this year.

TRAILMASTER

Yes, dammit. We'll maybe get less trouble from raiding parties. It'll weaken off their ponies sooner.

INDIAN SCOUT

Weaken we too.

TRAILMASTER

Quit that. Don't let me hear that kind of talk.

INDIAN SCOUT

Silver Heels no come.

TRAILMASTER

You've taken the money. That was the deal.

The INDIAN SCOUT takes out a small bag of gold dust and returns it to the TRAILMASTER.

ACT TWO

INDIAN SCOUT

Me no come. Snow too soon.

He slips off. The TRAILMASTER is worried.

ACT TWO SCENE SIX

At the Fork.

LEWIS (a forty-year old man), EMMA WEEKS, LIZZIE WEEKS, ANNIE WEEKS, JOSIAH WEEKS, MRS DOLAN, and MRS CARMODY are having an intense discussion.

LEWIS

I think we should take the cut-off. Can't be wrong to clip two hundred miles off the trail – tough trail at that.

EMMA

It's too risky.

MRS DOLAN

You agin it, Emma?

EMMA

I am.

MRS DOLAN

Then so am I.

The TRAILMASTER enters.

LIZZIE

What do you say, Mr Ames?

TRAILMASTER

What about?

ANNIE

Should we take the cut-off?

LEWIS

You bet!

EMMA

I say it's too risky. Why take chances?

TRAILMASTER

I'm inclined to favour Mrs Weeks.

LEWIS

You said yourself they saved ten days over the pass on the last trail. They took the cut-off!

TRAILMASTER

That's true.

MRS DOLAN

What makes you pause, Ethan?

TRAILMASTER

Lot of snow this year. Trail ain't so good on the cut-off. We could git snowed up.

LEWIS

It's worth the risk. Plenty of game up there. *(He pats his rifle.)* We won't go short. Plenty of meat for the children.

ANNIE

But if Ethan thinks we shouldn't risk it ...

MRS CARMODY

(To LEWIS)

We've our families to think of.

ACT TWO

LEWIS

We're aiming to shorten the hardship, Ma'am. That can't be a bad decision. Are you with us Ames?

TRAILMASTER

(Thinks, then, decisive.)

No, I'm not. We stick to the trail.

LEWIS

In that case, we split. You go by Fort Hall – we take the cut-off.

TRAILMASTER

I don't advise it.

LEWIS

We'll beat you into Sacramento.

TRAILMASTER

You're talking about people's lives, man!

LIZZIE

Ma?

MRS DOLAN

What do you think, Emma?

EMMA

I think it's foolishness. We've made it this far – no point taking chances now.

ANNIE

I agree!

JOSIAH

Hold on!

They turn and look at him. He says little now.

JOSIAH

The sooner we quit this harsh and miserable journey, the happier we shall be. *(To LEWIS.)* I shall join my party to your group, sir.

ANNIE

Pa!

LEWIS

Glad to have you, sir.

TRAILMASTER

Suit yourselves.

The group starts to break up.

EMMA

You're wrong Josiah. Dead wrong.

LIZZIE

Ma's right. We should stick to the trail.

JOSIAH

When I require your opinion, I'll ask for it. I'm still the head of this family.

LIZZIE

Of course you are, Pa.

JOSIAH

I suggest we begin to get our goods together ... *(Bitterly)* ... such as we have left to us.

Light change.

ACT TWO SCENE SEVEN

PEOPLE struggle, climbing. The calls and cries begin.

ACT TWO

VOICES

Quit the wagons! Abandon the wagons! Quit the wagons!

ACT TWO SCENE EIGHT

A SQUAW sits, mourning.

SQUAW

Cloud come down. Crow, sing song of death. Mud lies on the eyes of Canatego. Where are the Arapahoe? Where are the Pawnee? Chickasaw. Navaho. Apache! Shoshone ... Blackfoot ... Cherokeeeee ...

The INDIAN enters quietly, and stands beside her, exhausted.

INDIAN

I give myself up to you. Do with me what you please. Once I moved like the wind. Now I surrender to you, and that is all. We fought you as long as we had rifles. We have no provisions, no means to live. Your troops are everywhere; all our springs are overlooked by you ... by your young men. You have driven us out. We have no more heart. I hate all white people. You have taken away our lands. You have made us outcasts You do not know how to share.

SQUAW

Blood to water, water to stone, stone to ash. Farewell, Crow country.

ACT TWO SCENE NINE

In the snow.

OLAF

(Low, to EMMA)

She won't let go the baby.

EMMA

Leave her be. Let her carry it.

OLAF

It's frozen to her back. It'll kill her.

ACT TWO SCENE TEN

In the snow.

JOSIAH

I'm cold, I tell you. This morning, the ice was so heavy on my face, I couldn't speak. Where's your mother?

ANNIE

She went off with the squirrel gun.

JOSIAH

I can't even feel my feet.

ANNIE

You was wrong. We shouldn't have taken the cut-off. You should have listened to Ma.

JOSIAH

Where's Emma?

ANNIE

She'll be right along. God knows what we'll do if she comes back empty-handed. There ain't but a handful of corn flour.

ACT TWO

JOSIAH

Emma!

ACT TWO SCENE ELEVEN

In the snow.

Frozen bodies, huddled together. LEWIS enters, rifle in hand.

LEWIS

(Bends over a MAN)

Nothing.

MRS DE WITT

He's gone. Take his clothes. We shall have to bury him.

LEWIS

How are we going to do that?

He bends over the body.

LEWIS

This is meat.

MRS DE WITT

No. No.

LEWIS

I want to live.

MRS DE WITT

No.

Light change.

ACT TWO SCENE TWELVE

Twilight. Huddled bodies.

>> CRACKED VOICE

Another dead this morning. Pass it along.

>> VOICE

God forgive us.

Light change.

ACT TWO SCENE THIRTEEN

Day.

>> EMMA

She could of gotten down if she'd tried.

>> ANNIE

No, Ma. There was big falls during the night. Lizzie's all right. She's back up with the others. Lewis is there. He's a strong feller. He'll be keeping them all together.

>> EMMA

I'm worried. I've a mind to try ... If we don't do something soon, we'll be eating our own shoes.

>> ANNIE

They'll get down to us when they can. They'll make it to us. Pa? Pa?

>> EMMA

He won't last long. He's losing his will.

ACT TWO

ANNIE

If there's no more fall during the night, I'll try and get up to them.

EMMA

No. You stay with Pa. I'll go with the gun.

ACT TWO SCENE FOURTEEN

LIZZIE, alone, huddled for warmth. LEWIS enters silently with the rifle. He has hunted, rips off a piece of rabbit, and throws it to her.

They both eat. He throws it down in disgust. She looks at him.

LEWIS

It don't taste the same.

She gazes at him, frightened.

LEWIS

It don't taste the same!

LIZZIE is very alarmed. He looks mad.

Light change

ACT TWO SCENE FIFTEEN

EMMA

Tomorrow I'll make it. The snow's right off the big rock. I'll go back for her.

ANNIE

Let me go, Ma.

EMMA

She's my daughter. It's for me to find her. I'll go tomorrow.

JOSIAH

(He is very weak.)

Emma...

ACT TWO SCENE SIXTEEN

LEWIS

(Mutters)

It don't taste the same.

LIZZIE

Lewis, you wouldn't harm me, would you? If you harm me, you'll be alone.

LEWIS

I don't want to harm you. It just don't taste the same.

LIZZIE

Dear Lord, protect me. You wouldn't harm me, Lewis. That would be murder. The others died natural. God will forgive us for what we did. They'd have wanted us to live. Oh, dear God!

LEWIS

I don't mean to harm you. I got no quarrel with you.

LIZZIE

You can hunt. The relief party will be here any time now!

Her cry makes him draw off a little. But he watches her. Then he leans over and embraces her, as for warmth.

ACT TWO

LIZZIE

(Hope going.)

Don't harm me, Lewis. Don't harm me. Don't harm me.

LEWIS

I'll hunt tomorrow. I won't harm you.

LIZZIE

(Faint.)

Oh yes, you will. You're going to kill me.

LEWIS

No I ain't.

LIZZIE

(Sighs.)

Oh yes, you will. You're going to kill me.

LEWIS

It don't taste the same.

He clubs her with his rifle butt.

LEWIS

You see, Lizzie, it don't taste the same.

ACT TWO SCENE SIXTEEN

EMMA and ANNIE are sitting back to back, resting and eating, enjoying the warmth of the sun.

ANNIE

See that squirrel? Real tame. I was talking to the
old-timer back on the trail. He said when he was first
here, the animals was all real tame. Elk and deer'd
come right up and take a look in his pockets.

EMMA

They sure don't now.

ANNIE

They see you coming. Ma. Ain't nobody draws a bead like you.

EMMA

It's the knack of it. Always was far-sighted.

ANNIE

Best shot we had.

EMMA

Well maybe muh fingers was too small for the frost to take ... not so far for the blood to travel. I don't know.

She has no interest in speculation.

ANNIE

Funny how it was the women what survived. *(Pause.)* The birds have been acting strange.

EMMA

Hey! Kin you smell smoke?

ANNIE

That's odd. I thought I did. Just now.

EMMA

We can't be so far.

ANNIE

Reckon not.

They get up, get their gear together to move off.

Light change.

ACT TWO

ACT TWO SCENE SIXTEEN

A belvedere overlooking Sacramento.

A WELL-DRESSED MAN named ARCHER BURNETT enters, with his WIFE and her friend, MISS KITTY.

MRS BURNETT

How delightful! From here one may witness the whole golden magic of the West!

ARCHER

I told you the adventure would be worth the climb, my dear. What do you think of it, Miss Kitty?

MISS KITTY

Truly splendid. And this is all your land, Mr Burnett?

ARCHER

As far as the eye can see. And this is where the railroad will pass, straight as a gun barrel through the mountains to Omaha, St Louis, and the East.

MRS BURNETT

From coast to coast!

ARCHER

A week's travelling, instead of a year.

MISS KITTY

It will be a mighty fine achievement indeed.

ANNIE and EMMA approach. Neither party sees the other at first.

MRS BURNETT

Perhaps we could get the men to haul the picnic up here? Could you not command it, Archer? Why, I do believe I can see the spire of St James's Church. *(She sees ANNIE.)* Oh!

ARCHER

What the devil? In Heaven's name, what is it?
Pawnee, Sioux, wild woman or what? Come away,
ladies. I think it would be prudent to move our
ground.

They move away.

MISS KITTY
(Archly)

I read in the Examiner, Mr Burnett, that the ladies of
Wyoming are to have the vote.

ARCHER laughs heartily.

ARCHER

My dear Miss Kitty, can you imagine the suffrage in
the hands of such as we have just witnessed? Poor
abandoned creatures unable to fend for themselves?
No, my dears, the affairs of government and state must
be assigned to those equipped and designed for it.

MRS BURNETT

I'm sure I'm well content to leave our welfare in your
hands, my dear husband.

ARCHER

And you may be certain of my unceasing care and
protection, my love. An arm, ladies? *(They each take
an arm.)* A pleasure to escort two such decorative and
amiable companions.

They go.

ANNIE

Did I see it, or did I dream it? Ma ... Ma ...
civilisation! We made it. We made it!

ACT TWO

EMMA

(Approaches)

Made what?

ANNIE

We made it.

EMMA

My God. We're here. We are ... arrived.

They stare at Sacramento in the distance.

ANNIE

What happens now?

THE END.

THE WOMEN'S THEATRE COMPANY

The Beginning.

Sometime in the early 1970s, Ed Berman, the innovative American artistic director of the Almost Free Theatre in Rupert Street, London, W.1. (only Ed could have secured such a site in the heart of theatreland) had the idea of adapting a London bus and touring Camden – *the* lively Lefty area – performing plays on the top deck.

I had done one play – a pantomime at the cockpit Theatre called BETTY'S WONDERFUL CHRISTMAS – with a subtext about rape. Ed asked me for "two sexy pieces" for his Fun Art Bus.

I returned gun to holster and, to make a point, wrote hi two monologues: AFTER BIRTHDAY – about a girl on remand for shoving her new-born baby down the toilet of a mainline station – and MY WARREN, a piece about an exploited, overworked office drudge who is sent a vibrator by younger colleagues as a nasty joke and who – hating waste – uses it.

Ed didn't blink. He said they weren't quite what he had in mind but would produce them at the Almost Free.

This was achieved – not without stress. The male director of the first piece bowed out, finding it "too near the knuckle," and using a vibrator can present staging problems.

Thanks to two fine actresses – Sheila Kelly and Janet Henfrey – and rehearsing ourselves, we packed the theatre.

There was, just then, a hunger for plays about women.

These were the days of heroic neo-feminism, which had crossed the Atlantic from America, where women, ditched by burnt-out husbands after the period of six kid, two-car post-war triumphalism, were being forced to go it alone. Feminism on the continent followed England, and then spread, and is still spreading, thanks to the increasing value of women's labour.

After the success of the two plays, Ed Berman decided to mount a season of plays by women. A bunch of us set up a working group. We decided we wanted to run the whole show: direction, design, administration, lighting – these were the days when women, accustomed to carrying children inside and out, were considered too frail to lift stage-lights.

Ed Berman, possibly calling our bluff, said OK, but the theatre needed a paint-job. We painted it. We built a crèche in the scabby old basement, and made arrangements (probably illegal) to sell food in the foyer. This was the heyday of lunchtime theatre.

We received press attention, attracted many women interested in doing theatre, and formed a large committee. We met at my house, which had a large unfurnished room. Anyone who had written a play was invited to send it in. We had readings, sitting in a circle on beer crates. There was a great atmosphere, although the women who didn't have children, I remember, found them intrusive. Those of us with children merely raised our voices.

It wasn't easy to pick programme of plays. Many were impractical – "Enter a chorus of fifty nuns" – and some were so awful that a dreadful kindness reigned, misleading the poor authors who were bewildered when their plays were not short-listed.

Playwrighting – a practical craft – needs to be learned

on the job, and there was a lot of discussion as to how this could be achieved. Eventually, we selected a wonderfully mixed group of plays varied in style and content.

I submitted THE AMIABLE COURTSHIP OF MIZ VENUS AND WILD BILL, about an oaf and a harpy's attempts at equitable conjugality.

Lindsay Ingrams played Venus and Donald Sumpter played Wild Bill, and the production was lively. The season went well. We managed the crèche, made a profit on the veggie food and real lemon squash in the foyer, and received cordial notices. The Women's Theatre Group was formed.

It was an exciting time. There was more money about in those days, and Fringe Theatre was heady, pseudo-Marxist, and fashionable. Originality was welcomed. The mood was for the new. The Women's Theatre Group consolidated – and then split.

There was a dispute about libertarianism. Some women believed our doors should be open to all: old, young, British, non-British, gay, straight, short, tall, amateur and professional. Others believed we should include only professionals. After years of training, professional actresses suffering the poverty, insecurity, and unemployment associated with life in the theatre, became impatient with the casual attitudes of amateur members of the Women's Theatre Group. They were insulted by excuses like: "Didn't feel like it." "Had to see my boyfriend."

As a founder member, it was hard for me to leave the Women's Theatre Group, but I felt strongly that the professional theatre worker should be respected. Because we are all vocal and literate, there is a widespread belief that anyone can act or write, should the mood arise. Likewise, because theatre is 'entertainment,' there is, in England, the philistine belief that it's frivolous, extra-curricular, not important, its practitioners shallow and not to be regarded as contributing anything to society. In fact, the trained actor, dealing in depth with perception and the heart, plays a role as important as the clergyman, lawyer, or doctor.

The Women's Theatre Group split and a second collective made up of professional theatre workers formed itself into The Women's Theatre Company. Both groups applied to the Arts Council, and the Women's Theatre Company was successful.

Our first show was my play GO WEST YOUNG WOMAN, which opened at the Round House in 1974. This did well, apart from the first night, when two groups of women hardliners, who objected to the presence of men in the cast, tried to storm the stage and destroy the set.

However, the initial success of the Women's Theatre Company wasn't followed up. There were Arts Council cuts and funding issues. The climate grew bleaker. There were difficulties holding a core group together when the choice is to play a feminist Medea for no money, or a hairdresser in a soap opera. Most actresses don't have rich partners, or parents, to subsidise them.

Wonderfully, the Women's Theatre Company survived and became Sphinx. Perhaps it should be Phoenix!

There is so much need for work by women about women for women. Society is changing so quickly that everything – identity, purpose, raison d'etre – is in question. This is the first generation that women have been effectively freed from the severe dangers of childbirth, and have access to education. Whether they wish it or not, women are now existential. Like men, they have to make themselves up. Both men and women are endowed with new freedoms, and assailed by new insecurities. More than ever now, released from the stabilities of slavery, we – all of us – need a healthy, jaunty, vigorous theatre, popular, gritty, and for everyone.

Pam Gems

KING LUDWIG OF BAVARIA

LUDWIG II

KING LUDWIG OF BAVARIA

CHARACTERS

KING LUDWIG II OF BAVARIA

EMPRESS ELISABETH OF AUSTRIA (SISSI)

CAPTAIN FREDERICK VON EBERHARDT

KING LUDWIG OF BAVARIA

ACT ONE

ACT ONE SCENE ONE

(Optional.)

[On the front cloth, projected footage of Prussian and Austro-Hungarian march-pasts in full panoply – with cavalry, foot soldiers and heavy guns. On the soundtrack: martial music, loud and discordant, and barked military commands. The sounds die to silence.

LUDWIG, King of Bavaria, in full regalia, enters stage left. He pauses, nods in response to his people, traverses, and stares out at the audience, unsmiling.

At the same time SISSI, the Empress of Austria, enters stage right. She is magnificently dressed in a full evening dress with diamonds and a small diamond crown. She receives the applause of the crowd with a gentle hand gesture, and a warm smile. The two cross the stage. As they pass each other, they exchange a small friendly smile and touch hands briefly.

They exit.]

Lights up on the interior of a detached HUNTING LODGE.

Though simple in style, it is well appointed, with signs of regal splendour. There is a glowing log fire, comfortable seating, and side tables. On one of the tables is a LARGE SWAN made of ice holding an ornate dish of oysters, with knives to open them. Upstage is a long, narrow table with a white damask cloth, appointed with crystal and flowers, and laden with food, including a dressed boar's head.

It is Late afternoon. Sound of voices, offstage.

LUDWIG enters, waving someone away.

LUDWIG

No, no, no, no, no!

CAPTAIN VON EBERHARDT follows him in, wearing an ornate pale brown uniform.

LUDWIG

Not outside the door, not on the verandah, not on the steps!

EBERHARDT

With due respect ...

LUDWIG

I order you and the rest of your louts to freeze your undoubtedly inadequate parts ...

EBERHARDT

Sire!

LUDWIG

... at the end of the lane, by the gate and no closer. Where are the oysters?

EBERHARDT

Oysters?

LUDWIG

The oysters! Where are the oysters?

EBERHARDT

Behind you.

ACT ONE

LUDWIG

(Turns and sees them.)

Put a thug on the gate to wave a lantern when the carriage arrives.

EBERHARDT

I must protest!

LUDWIG:

What? What? What did you say?

EBERHARDT

My men and I are in charge of your protection.

LUDWIG

And I am ordering you to clear off.

EBERHARDT

I beg your pardon, Sire. But may I implore you to allow a small detachment around the lodge, out of sight? They won't be heard or seen ...

LUDWIG

No, no, no, no, no, no, no, no, no! Linderhof and the forest around for miles are ring-fenced with your ugly faces – isn't that enough? I don't want you in my sight! Do I make myself clear?

EBERHARDT

Sire.

LUDWIG

Outside! Outside the gate. You are to stand under the trees. Keep out of sight. I don't want her to see a single soldier ... she hates soldiers. Wave the lantern for the coachman, open the gates, and swing the lantern high so I know she's coming. When the coachman returns, close the gates after him and no one – no one is to approach – do you hear me?

EBERHARDT
(Sulky)
Yes, Sire. I hear you. Sire.

LUDWIG
And I will not have you in that ludicrous brown. You look like the platoon privy – where is the blue?

EBERHARDT
Almost ready, Sire.

LUDWIG
Well hurry them up or I'll have you all on parade bollock-naked.

EBERHARDT
(Sullen)
As Your Majesty wishes.

LUDWIG glares at the possible impertinence, but decides to let it go. The CAPTAIN bows and leaves – pausing at the door.

EBERHARDT
The snow's thickening. Would you like me to have the steps cleared?

LUDWIG
No.

EBERHARDT
It's half-way up the …

LUDWIG
Get out!

CAPTAIN VON EBERHARDT goes. LUDWIG strides about, irritated.

ACT ONE

> LUDWIG
> *(Mutters)*

No, no, no, no, no.

He crosses, looks at himself in the glass, straightens his jacket, and picks a flower from an elaborate arrangement of gardenias.

He smells it, and puts it in his buttonhole. He looks in the mirror – decides against it – and throws the flower at the fire. Then he rescues the flower and cradles it. He pours water into a wine glass and places the flower into it.

> LUDWIG
> *(To the flower)*

Forgive me.

He inspects the food – rearranges two dishes. Then he goes to the mirror again, and smooths his hair.

A CLOCK chimes four. He smiles, and shakes his head.

> LUDWIG

She will – of course – be late.

> SISSI

Slanderer.

SISSI is in the doorway, smothered in furs, with a pale silk gauze scarf over her hair. He turns, and goes to her. She enfolds him in her arms for a long moment.

> LUDWIG

Vereint sind Liebe und Lenz.

> SISSI

Liebling … belovéd.

> LUDWIG

My dearest, dearest friend – my light – I was afraid that you wouldn't –

SISSI

I know.

LUDWIG

They told me.

SISSI

I know.

LUDWIG

You got here safely?

SISSI

Yes. You've sent all the soldiers away?

LUDWIG

Of course.

SISSI

Thank you.

She kisses the top of his head, pulls back and inspects him.

LUDWIG

Well?

SISSI

For someone surrounded by a regiment of vipers you look surprisingly well.

LUDWIG

I'm in face today. Bien dans la peau.

SISSI

Absolument. You look adorable.

LUDWIG

Comme toujours, but ... ?

ACT ONE

He pats his face in enquiry. She walks around him on a tour of inspection. She pauses to sniff the gardenias, smiles her thanks. Regards him keenly, and nods.

SISSI

The regime has worked.

He pats his flat midriff, gratified, and helps her off with her furs.

She removes the gauze scarf from her head, then crosses to the glass to arrange her magnificent Titian hair – scattering haircombs. He grovels at her feet, picking them up. She turns to display her new ensemble.

LUDWIG

Paris?

SISSI

Of course.

LUDWIG

And designed by Worth?

SISSI

Bien sur. Made in three days by poor little midinettes ruining their eyes so I should look decent for you.

He inspects her, nods.

LUDWIG

Bravo, les petites. May they have long and fabulous lives.

SISSI

Not so fabulous to sew through two and a half nights.

LUDWIG

For the Empress? Whom they adore? Ecstasy.

She smiles at him, and he escorts her to a seat, putting a Rococo stool under her feet. He fetches a large wolf skin rug, puts it over her knees and places a cushion behind her head.

LUDWIG

He bends over her, kisses her hair. (*He touches her temple.*) No more pain here?

SISSI

Not as much.

LUDWIG

And the hip?

SISSI

Brutal. But I rode yesterday.

LUDWIG

No, no, no, no, no, no, no, no! You could take a fall!

SISSI

Into delicious deep snow ...

LUDWIG

Not necessarily. Stay in the warm!

He attends to the fire, which blazes up. She looks down at his bent shoulders.

SISSI

(*Gently*)

How are you, dearest?

He looks up at her, holding an eloquent glance.

SISSI

I expected to find you in Munich.

LUDWIG

To hear the annual list of complaints?

ACT ONE

SISSI

They say they can't pay the army.

LUDWIG

It's my money. I can do as I please. I AM the King! Anything new?

SISSI

(Shakes her head)

The usual. Linderhof was acceptable as a royal folly, but Neuschwanstein ...

LUDWIG

Oh, not still! I never go near it. I hate the place!

SISSI

Then why did you spend all that time and money building it?

LUDWIG

(Shrugs)

I was depressed.

SISSI

It's the most lyrical castle!

LUDWIG

From the outside. Inside, a punitive retreat for the deranged. I shall never use oak again.

SISSI

They're worried about the new one on the lake.

LUDWIG

Herrenchiemsee? Why can't they understand? Building on an island is bound to cost more! *(Pause)* There must be a way to grow orange trees out of doors. Oh damn! It was meant to be a surprise for you.

They say lemons are easier. I thought pipes – miles
of hot pipes. Oranges growing in the snow. Would you
like that?

SISSI

Wonderful. *(She takes his hands.)* They're looking to
Uncle Otto.

LUDWIG

Uncle Otto?

SISSI

To replace you.

LUDWIG

Uncle Otto? Who wears his shoes on the wrong feet –
served me boiled beef and onions and, all the way
through an increasingly tragic menu, talked about
drains.

SISSI laughs.

LUDWIG

That wasn't the half of it! After chocolate cannonballs
in blood sauce, he insisted – yet again – that I look at
his collection.

SISSI

Of mortars and ramrods. I've seen them. We must
resist Uncle Otto.

LUDWIG

How? With what?

SISSI

Charm?

ACT ONE

LUDWIG

Gottverdammt! If I choose to spend on beauty rather than death and weapons, are they sane, or am I? I am building for delight.

SISSI

And for the future.

LUDWIG

They don't see it that way.

SISSI

Do you expect them to?

He ponders this.

LUDWIG

No, no, no, no, no, no, no, no, no, of course not.

A comfortable pause.

SISSI

I hear Wagner has been dismissed again.

LUDWIG

You hear correctly.

SISSI

May one know why?

LUDWIG

His own fault.

SISSI

It always is. Not another abortion for the mistress?
LUDWIG:

(Shakes his head)

No, no, no. The man is a – he's nothing but a greedy, grasping arschgeige.

SISSI

Are you speaking?

LUDWIG

Not at the moment. No. Finished.

SISSI

Forgive him, darling. Make up.

LUDWIG

I think not.

SISSI

Please. For me? For me.

LUDWIG

And you'll make my life a misery if I don't.

SISSI

A nest of cobras!

She waves her arms at him like a snake charmer.

LUDWIG

He'll have to find some sublime chord sequences.

SISSI

Which he will. And thanks to your generous heart we shall have a splendid new opera and the world will be a richer place.

LUDWIG

And I shall be bankrupt.

SISSI

Guten Kaufs macht den Beutel leer – buying well empties the purse.

LUDWIG

That I can confirm.

ACT ONE

SISSI

Let me see. You can't get rid of the horses. The Royal plate?

LUDWIG

Already pledged.

SISSI

Good, it's hideous. The Crown Jewels?

LUDWIG

Also hideous.

SISSI

Then you won't miss them.

LUDWIG

The Cellini epergne will have to go.

SISSI

Never mind.

LUDWIG

Oh, wär ich nie geboren.

He rises and crosses to the side table. She turns to see him with a dangerous-looking knife in his hands.

SISSI

Darling, you're not going to kill us both?

LUDWIG

And deprive the rest of Bavaria of that pleasure?

SISSI

(Not amused.)

Don't.

LUDWIG

Sorry.

                    SISSI

You aren't careful enough.

                    LUDWIG

What?

                    SISSI

You go about incognito, but everybody knows who you are!

                    LUDWIG

No, they don't.

                    SISSI

They do! Your face is on every pfennig! Darling, there's no excuse. If you were stupid – but you're not. Must I remind you, in your position, it is normal to be in danger. We both are, it's the royal condition. It goes with the wave from the balcony, the sapphires and the pearls.

                    LUDWIG
          (Presenting the ornate dish of heaped oysters.)
The knife is for these.

SISSI throws up her hands in pleasure.

                    SISSI

Oysters!

He does a turn, the dish held high. She claps.

                    SISSI

Darling, darling boy – you always remember!

                    LUDWIG

Brittany. We walked on the beach ...

                    SISSI

– without shoes –

ACT ONE

LUDWIG

... and the wind took your hair and it streamed behind you like a flock of flamingoes.

SISSI

Flamingoes?!

LUDWIG

Unique, adorable creatures.

SISSI

With legs that go backwards.

LUDWIG

Golden orioles then.

He attacks the oysters.

SISSI

Do be careful. Why weren't they opened for you?

He gives her a brief smile, opens an oyster, lays it on the plate, then chooses a second, opens it, inspects it, puts it in the palm of his hand and brings it to her. She smiles up at him, frowning in puzzlement. And looks down at the oyster.

SISSI

Oh Ludo! A pearl!

LUDWIG

An enormous pearl.

SISSI

My dear...

He picks out the pearl from the oyster, rinses it in his mouth, wipes it clean on his lace cuff, drops it into her open hand, and eats the oyster.

                    SISSI

           A pearl. A pink pearl!

They inspect it together.

                    LUDWIG

           Probably the light from the fire.

He begins to open more oysters.

                    SISSI

           More?

She rises and joins him.

                    LUDWIG

           There'd better be.

He opens oysters. She takes a knife and they both open an oyster, eating them as they go. He pours wine and they drink in between.

                    LUDWIG

                Here's another!

She picks out the pearl, swills it in her mouth and inspects it.

                    SISSI

                (Showing him)

           I found one! Even bigger!

But another pearl in his mouth distracts him. He frowns, taking it out and peering at it.

                    SISSI

           What's the matter?

                    LUDWIG

           There's something wrong with this one. It's gritty on
           the tongue.

ACT ONE

SISSI

Dearest, that's how you know pearls are genuine.

They feed each other one more oyster each. Then they wash their hands. He dries hers, she dries his. He brings the dish of pearls, places them on her lap.

SISSI

One, two, three, four, five! And so large! Where are they from?

LUDWIG

The South Seas.

SISSI

Oh, to be there!

LUDWIG

Yes. Warm sand – palm trees – blue ocean. Just you and me – and Peko of course. *(He looks round)* Where is Peko?

SISSI

I didn't bring him.

LUDWIG

Why ever not?

SISSI

You're jealous of him.

LUDWIG

True.

SISSI

How can you be jealous of a little dog?

LUDWIG

He has bigger eyes and a prettier tail than me.

SISSI plays with the pearls.

                    SISSI

Five pearls.

                    LUDWIG

Oh – I forgot.

He jumps up, takes a large SUEDE BAG from his jacket pocket. And pours a river of pearls into her lap.

                    LUDWIG

Happy anniversary!

He slides beside her on the wide seat and they kiss tenderly.

                    SISSI

Oh, my darling ... (*They kiss again.*) So many
years ...

                    LUDWIG

From my first vision of you across the parade ground
on the grey ...

                    SISSI

I was riding Nightfall –

                    LUDWIG

And I helped you down –

                    SISSI

... and caught my heel in the stirrup ...

                    LUDWIG

... and we looked in each other's eyes –

                    SISSI

And there it was.

                    LUDWIG

There we were.

ACT ONE

SISSI

You were me.

LUDWIG

And I was you. *(Slight pause.)* So strange. Inconvenient.

SISSI

Inconvenient?

LUDWIG

Poor timing. You'd already been sold off to that old lecher.

SISSI

Ssh...

LUDWIG

... that dreadful, diseased old lecher.

SISSI

Please don't.

LUDWIG

Why not? It's true.

SISSI

I feel sorry for him.

LUDWIG

Sorry? For your destroyer? You're not saying you forgive him?

SISSI

I must dearest, otherwise I am destroyed.

LUDWIG

There's no forgiveness. He has tainted your body. I should like to throw him into a vat of hot metal.

                    SISSI

Don't.

                    LUDWIG

Watch his eyes as he looks up with one last agonized
glare.

                    SISSI

Stop it.

He picks up pearls from the floor, she scoops them from her lap.
They pour them back into the suede bag. He pulls her to her feet.

                    LUDWIG

Come and choose.

He leads her by the hand to the table laden with food and wine.

She bends to smell the gardenias again. He gestures to the food.

                    SISSI

Delicious!

                    LUDWIG

And all for you.

                    SISSI

Every little bit?

LUDWIG nods.

                    SISSI

Promise?

                    LUDWIG

Cross my heart.

                    SISSI
                (Prowling the food)

Oh, your heart –

ACT ONE

LUDWIG

What do you mean – my heart?

SISSI

Hardly stable currency.

LUDWIG

Hah! A gold coin for every female fickle fish in this room.

SISSI

Touché. But there it is. I am fickle, therefore I am.

LUDWIG

A retreat to the Cartesian is no absolution.

SISSI

"Il est bien difficile enfin d'être fidèle
A de certains maris faits d'un certain modèle."
Don't expect me to pursue virtue. At least not yet.
(They laugh.) You have made us a feast.

LUDWIG

Let me be your maitre. *(He takes her arm, walks her along the table.)* Wild boar – as you see.

SISSI

With a less than charmed expression.

LUDWIG

Unsurprisingly.

SISSI

But stoic.

LUDWIG

That's because he sits in a blueberry and wild garlic sauce on a bed of champignons and fleurettes de something or other in your honour ... Or there's venison, marinaded for a week in walnut oil and lime juice, with red-currant and jus d'orange sauces. Sweetbreads à la mode ... carp à la Polonaise – lemon sole au natural avec pommes vapeur and haricots vert – lobster of course – caviar – foie de veau – No, no, no, no, no! I expressly said no pommes frites! *(Throws the dish casually in the fire.)* What an insult! I'm so sorry.

SISSI

Dear boy – delicious! *(She bends and sniffs a dish)* Unborn lamb?

LUDWIG

With apricots.

SISSI

And sage.

LUDWIG

And sage.

SISSI

Now how can that be? Only Armand uses sage. No one else would dare.

LUDWIG

A skewer to the heart if they did.

SISSI

Then – where did you – how did you? By rail? Days on ice?

LUDWIG

I wouldn't dream of offering you luggage as food.

SISSI

Then how on earth -?

ACT ONE

LUDWIG

I sent for him.

SISSI

For Armand? Armand himself? From Paris? You're teasing me. He would never leave the quartier.

LUDWIG

Except for you.

He kisses her hand and they look at Armand's special dish.

SISSI

Beautiful. Utterly, utterly beautiful. You will thank him for me?

LUDWIG

I already have.

SISSI

With some little gift?

LUDWIG

A small chateau near Aix. From us both. With a fortified tower.

SISSI

Fortified?

LUDWIG

Against thieves. His recipes!

SISSI

Ah, of course! *(Smiles.)* You're mad – fou!

LUDWIG

So the world tells me.

SISSI

And I am folle. Thank God. *(She prowls the table.)* All for me ... all for me ...

He puts a napkin on one arm.

LUDWIG

Madame desires?

SISSI

Oh, everything. Mmmm ... Let me see. The carp?

LUDWIG

Accompanied by seared whitebait, with crevettes au beurre blanc?

SISSI

Or a little of this? A bowl of -? No – a simple coq au vin with quenelles? Or ... Mmm ... you have presented me with a challenge, chéri.

LUDWIG

Un peu de viande? – ah, the ormers!

SISSI

Such a shame to destroy the ensemble.

LUDWIG

It shall rot away in your honour.

SISSI

Ah.

LUDWIG

Ah?

SISSI

I think –

ACT ONE

LUDWIG

Yes?

SISSI

Perhaps?

LUDWIG

Yes?

SISSI

A soupçon of lemon sorbet – in a little white dish.

LUDWIG

Perfect choice.

He dishes out one tablespoon of sorbet into a white dish, puts it on a gold plate and crosses, waits for her to sit, and then places it on her lap, with the napkin to hand for her.

SISSI

Wicked boy, that's far too much!

He laughs.

LUDWIG

Forgive me.

He watches her fondly as she puts the spoon to her lips. He puts a light shawl on her shoulders – adds a log to the fire, crosses, and looks out of the window. The wind begins to rise.

LUDWIG

More snow.

SISSI

Delicious.

She puts the plate and spoon aside, having eaten nothing.

LUDWIG

Perhaps we shall be marooned?

SISSI

Good.

She joins him at the window.

LUDWIG

There's plenty of wood outside –

SISSI

And food. And we'll be safe! If no one can reach us, we'll be safe. *(They look at each other and out at the snow.)* I am so frightened.

LUDWIG

Don't be.

SISSI

I worry about you.

LUDWIG

No, no, no – waste of time.

SISSI

But I –

He puts a finger against her lips.

LUDWIG

Ssh. Look!

The snow is higher against the windowpane.

SISSI

Oh! We're going to be smothered! In a snow house! *(Murmurs)* Das Wunderreich der Nacht. How I love winter!

LUDWIG

Du bist der Lenz.

They embrace.

ACT ONE

ACT ONE SCENE TWO

SISSI and LUDWIG are playing draughts, a small table between them. He beats her with seven triumphant moves, clearing the board. Maddened, she throws the whole lot in the air.

>LUDWIG

I won.

>SISSI

You cheated!

>LUDWIG

You can't cheat at draughts.

>SISSI

Yes, you can!

>LUDWIG

How?

>SISSI

By going like this. *(She imitates his rapid clearing of the board)* So I can't see what you are doing.

>LUDWIG

Rubbish, you saw every move! I went –

He imitates his movements in a studied manner.

>LUDWIG

How could you not see that?

Maddeningly, he does it again.

>SISSI

My eyes are bad, you take advantage. That's cheating.

LUDWIG

The King of Bavaria is not, has never been, nor will ever be a cheat. He is deeply insulted and demands his pearls back.

SISSI

The King of Bavaria can go to Siberia.

LUDWIG

Now you're for it.

He chases and catches her and they roll on the floor. He holds her firmly.

SISSI

You – have a very, very cruel streak. Cruel knees and cruel feet and cruel hair.

LUDWIG

I am the mildest, most humane, sweetest-tempered man in the civilised world and you know it.

SISSI

Then why were you so vile to Paul?

A heavy silence.

LUDWIG

Shall we not talk about that?

SISSI

You mean you daren't.

LUDWIG

Not at all.

SISSI

Because you're ashamed.

ACT ONE

LUDWIG

I am not.

SISSI

Ashamed of the way you behaved.

LUDWIG

No.

SISSI

All Europe is talking.

LUDWIG

So, now I'm King Pédé. Bravo.

SISSI

Better than being King Dimwit – well, that title is already taken. I'm married to him.

Silence

LUDWIG

I didn't behave badly.

SISSI

You were vile.

LUDWIG

Je l'ai trop aimé pour ne point haïr.

SISSI

You humiliated him. Publicly. Was that necessary?

LUDWIG

Absolutely.

SISSI

Why?

LUDWIG

Revenge.

SISSI

There you are – in your own mouth. Revenge.

LUDWIG

Deliberate. And public. Pour décourager les autres. I will not have vipers in my household. He can eat dirt and enjoy it – Staub soll er fressen, und mit Lust. Rache ist mein Gewerbe.

SISSI

And you know who is reliable – faithful to you?

LUDWIG

Of course not. I was a fool. I fell in love. Ridiculous. It always ends badly.

SISSI

Yes.

He grasps her hand, briefly.

LUDWIG

We both suffer the hours spent listening to flattery knowing that you will never be liked, loved for yourself.

SISSI

That's always true for women. When I was fifteen, I cut off my hair and wore black, so they'd love me for the real me.

LUDWIG

And did they?

SISSI

Of course not!

A loud, dull, heavy sound. She starts. He puts a protective arm around her.

ACT ONE

LUDWIG

It's the snow, falling from the roof. Come by the fire –
I'll fetch more wood.

He goes to the door, opens it, and snow falls in. The doorway is completely covered in driven snow. She joins him.

LUDWIG

The wind's driven the drifts onto the verandah.

LUDWIG goes to the window, now covered by snow.

LUDWIG

We are snowed in!

SISSI

Bravo. Thank you, snow! *(She throws snow into the air.)* Thank you, blissful, delicious snow. You are my chevalier servant – my second-best friend.

LUDWIG

They'll have us out soon enough ...

SISSI

I daresay.

LUDWIG

... with you here, my badge of safety. *(Hugs her.)* We must keep warm. Food! We'll eat.

SISSI

Why not?

She prowls, inspecting the room. She sees a pile of scripts, picks up the top script, flicks open the first page and reads.

SISSI

"A glass of your good Rhenish wine, mein Herr!" *(She gestures with the script)* What is this? *(She looks at the cover.)* A new opera?

LUDWIG

Yes, yes.

SISSI

Not by Wagner?

LUDWIG

No, no, no, no, no, no, no. Just one more contender for his place. They arrive daily.

SISSI

(Reads the title)

'Das Weib ist Schön' – Women are Beautiful. It sounds rather jolly.

LUDWIG

Be careful or I shall play you the music.

He brings a platter of food and napkins and they sit side by side under the wolf rug. He rises, pours and brings wine. She drinks.

LUDWIG

Spiced peaches? Have one – just for me.

She takes one – eats obediently. They eat in silence. The wind rises outside. He removes the food and they lie, cuddled together.

Candlelight lower.

SISSI

(Shudders)

Ugh – cold, liebling.

LUDWIG

I'll burn the furniture.

SISSI

No, don't do that.

ACT ONE

LUDWIG

Then I'll keep you warm. *(He cuddles her close.)* Shall I make love to you?

SISSI

Will that help?

LUDWIG

We'll keep it in reserve. Unless I get too cold to manage anything.

They cuddle and look at the fire. She looks at his profile.

SISSI

You look sad.

LUDWIG

Ich bin mein Himmel und meine Hölle.

SISSI

Don't. *(She takes his hand.)* Have you been writing?

LUDWIG

No. There'll be no more poetry. My lyric phase, it seems, is over.

SISSI

To be replaced by more majestic imaginations.

LUDWIG

(Laughs)

Now they will do me in.

SISSI

We must lie low. *(They snuggle together. Pause.)* Ludo?

LUDWIG

Mmmm?

SISSI

Do you love me?

He turns to her in surprise.

LUDWIG

Yes.

SISSI

Am I your friend?

LUDWIG

Yes. My best friend. My only friend.

SISSI

Do you trust me?

He looks at her – a momentary panic. He dismisses it.

LUDWIG

I trust you with my life.

SISSI

Darling – go to Vienna. Give way on something... just something – the army...

LUDWIG

The army? That vat of abattoir meat?

SISSI

The secret service then.

LUDWIG

No! Why should I support a phalanx of cross-eyed idiots whose wives would frighten every parrot in Brazil from its tree?

SISSI

To keep them on your side. To keep you safe. Work up a few favourites. Set one general against another.

ACT ONE

>Ridicule one spy, elevate another – create regal
>havoc. Divide and rule. You must do something!

He fidgets with his hair.

LUDWIG

Why?

SISSI

Because, if you are killed ...

She is overcome by emotion. A pause. Then he lifts his hand up to her, and grasps hers.

LUDWIG

You've forgotten our agreement. Never to give way to melancholy ... remember?

SISSI

I know, I know, I know – but the feelings against you in Vienna frighten me.

LUDWIG

There is no need for that. None at all.

SISSI

But the mood is so ...

LUDWIG

I tell you it doesn't matter. None of it matters. I won't be touched. Believe me.

SISSI

Why not? Plenty of precedent for regicide – for usurping a king.

LUDWIG

Sissi. Look at me. I – will – not – be – touched.

SISSI

How do you know?

LUDWIG

Because no one will dare.

SISSI

They will!

LUDWIG

No, they won't.

SISSI

Why not?

LUDWIG

Because they can't. Shall I tell you why? Bismarck likes me.

SISSI

Bismarck? Is he –? Bismarck?

LUDWIG

Why do you think Bavaria exists – this pimple of a country? Why haven't we been – *(He makes a slurping sound)* – swallowed – erased from the map of Europe? While I keep my looks – which I intend to do – I am safe, and Bavaria is safe and what more can a ruler be expected to provide for his loyal, devoted and grateful subjects?

Silence.

SISSI

Are you sure?

LUDWIG

Yes. *(He cuddles her.)* How are the pigeons?

ACT ONE

               SISSI

Proliferating.

               LUDWIG

Still pink?

               SISSI

Still pink.

               LUDWIG

And Peko?

               SISSI

Still bald.

               LUDWIG

You tried the aloe?

               SISSI

Yes! Thank you! The skin is much less cracked – though his poor little paws are as poignant as ever.

               LUDWIG

Still has to be carried?

               SISSI

Everywhere.

The candles are lower.

               SISSI

Are you asleep?

               LUDWIG
               (Jerking awake)

No. Shall I do it to you now? Would you like that?

               SISSI

Will it make us warmer?

LUDWIG

Yes, I think so. Probably.

SISSI

But is your heart in it, liebling?

LUDWIG

You know I've always loved you.

SISSI

So much that you'd risk syphilis? I am a diseased person.

LUDWIG

Do you think I care about that? It would be a privilege.

SISSI

No. Don't ask for syphilis.

LUDWIG

What difference does it make? I shall be dead long before the tertiary stage.

SISSI

Oh please, please don't talk like that, I can't bear it when you talk like that.

Pause. She stirs, restless.

LUDWIG

Sissi?

SISSI

Relax, my dearest darling – it's not a sport we favour, either of us. Der Körper ist nicht das ganze Tier ... the body is not the entire animal.

ACT ONE

LUDWIG

At least, as a woman, you can lie back. Men are supposed to be king of the castle, cock of the walk –

SISSI

Oh, women hate all that.

LUDWIG

They do? Truly?

SISSI

Yes.

LUDWIG

Thank God. *(Slight pause.)* What do they like?

SISSI

Tenderness. To feel protected. And a man who can make them laugh.

He jumps up, does animal imitations. She laughs and applauds and he joins her and they cuddle.

SISSI

I'm glad we're not going to do it.

LUDWIG

Could spoil everything.

SISSI

I'm not sure it wouldn't come under the heading of incest. Suppose we had a child? With two heads ...

LUDWIG

So long as they both looked like you.

They cuddle.

SISSI

Sleepy?

LUDWIG

A little.

She sings him a verse of a lullaby.

LUDWIG

Lovely ... lovely.

SISSI

And because I truly love you I shan't perform an encore.

LUDWIG

(Kisses her hair)

You have a beautiful voice –

She nestles in his arms, and then moves, restless. She sits up, looks down at him.

SISSI

All this talk of sex. What do you do when you feel restless?

LUDWIG

Think of higher things.

She barks with laughter.

SISSI

I pleasure myself. Where's the harm, you damage no one, don't you agree?

LUDWIG

Who knows? I'm too terrified most days. Daily doses of fright put ardour to flight.

SISSI

Despite your powerful protector? *(She embraces him)* Oh, my dear love.

ACT ONE

They cuddle. The candles are very low.

SISSI

Did I tell you – I bought the Murillo?

LUDWIG

(Excited)

The big one – with the tiger?

SISSI

Have it.

LUDWIG

Be careful, I might say yes.

SISSI

I shall have it shipped to you tomorrow.

LUDWIG

Lend it to me. Ach! *(As she hugs him.)* I've been out on the slopes, sledging.

SISSI

Ludo, no! You promised!

LUDWIG

Dearest, it's wonderful. You're so free – so alone – so alive on a sledge!

SISSI

Till you hit a tree.

LUDWIG

Do you listen to me when I tell you not to ride?

SISSI

No.

LUDWIG

There you are then.

Pause.

SISSI

Are you sleepy?

She murmurs a tune.

LUDWIG

Don't stop.

SISSI

Go to sleep.

LUDWIG

No. Sing to me – I don't want to miss a second of you.

She sings a song from Schubert's Wintereisse.

LUDWIG

Thank you.

They cuddle.

LUDWIG

You are the light of my life. *(Sits up abruptly.)* I have it!

SISSI

Dearest?

LUDWIG

It was there – in my brain. I knew – I knew – *(He laughs, excited.)* Oh, I have such a surprise for you! No, I can't wait, I must tell you, you'll find out anyway. It'll take years to build.

SISSI

Build what?

LUDWIG:

Don't look so alarmed – not our mausoleums.

ACT ONE

SISSI

What?

LUDWIG

The Forbidden Palace. Peking. The Forbidden Palace, in the Chinese style throughout, from one mile's end to the other ... On the border between Bavaria and Austria so we can meet more easily. Think of it Sissi – our own Chinese Palace! Utterly authentic – Chinese silks – Chinese food. What do they eat? It can't all be birds' nest soup and hundred-year-old eggs. Don't you think it's a good idea?

SISSI

(Sleepy)

A wonderful idea.

LUDWIG

I shall need Chinese designers – architects –

SISSI

Mmmm.

LUDWIG

And you must have those little slippers with no heels.

SISSI

But not on the wrong feet like Uncle Otto.

LUDWIG

Oh, your enchanting feet will be bound – you'll only be able to hobble. I shall have to carry you.

SISSI

(Sleepy)

Splendid ... *(Pause.)* We will be rescued? They will come for us?

LUDWIG

Yes. Unless after a plenary session it is decided that Bavaria and Austria will be inestimably improved by a suffocation of snow.

SISSI

Would they – truly – do that?

LUDWIG

Where there is a Prussian, there is murder.

SISSI

And we are surrounded by them! How can one take a breath without being afraid?

LUDWIG

Ssh. Go to sleep.

The candles go out. There is silence. Cracking sounds of the weight of snow on the roof. And then silence.

A long pause. And then a SHOT – very loud. SISSI and LUDWIG jerk awake and she screams. He leaps for his gun on the side table.

A RUMBLING NOISE of snow falling from the roof.

SISSI

Goodbye, my darling. *(She kisses him.)*

LUDWIG

Farewell, Beloved.

SISSI

At least we're together.

BANGING from above. LUDWIG stands bravely, protecting SISSI. He jumps aside, takes down an ornamental sword.

The banging continues. Then there are loud, cracking sounds as a hole is hacked through the wooden roof. A stream of sunlight.

ACT ONE

> LUDWIG

Is that you, Fritz?

> EBERHARDT

Ludo, are you alive?

> LUDWIG

Of course I'm bloody alive! Dig us out!

> EBERHARDT

We had to fire a round to dislodge the snow. We're digging our way to the door. Is her Serene Highness safe?

> LUDWIG

She's bloody cold – we both are!

> EBERHARDT

Hang on Sire! *(Aside)* Hurry up, there, with the fire! Come on, their Majesties are freezing!

Noises from above – then a brazier of live coals is lowered. LUDWIG reaches for his gloves, releases and shakes the chain, and the chain is retrieved. He holds out his hands to SISSI. She retrieves hers from her fur muff and he rubs them briskly.

They hold out their hands over the glowing coals. Outside, voices, and sounds of the men digging.

> SISSI

We're safe.

> LUDWIG

I daresay.

> SISSI

They're here to save us! We're safe!

LUDWIG

(Shrugs.)

Did you think we weren't?

SISSI

We both did.

LUDWIG

Yes. Such an excuse for two splendid funerals – black-plumed horses – kings, queens, princes – what a deprivation. I've already chosen my order of service. Wagner, but not exclusively ...

SISSI

Stop it.

They stand, looking down at the fire, arm in arm.

LUDWIG

Safe.

They look at each other as the sounds increase outside the door.

The door begins to be pushed open and snow falls in. She grasps him, and holds him firmly.

LUDWIG

It's all right. They won't harm us.

SISSI

They will.

LUDWIG

Sssh.

SISSI

Promise never to let them kill you.

LUDWIG

I promise.

ACT ONE

SISSI

Please ...

LUDWIG

I promise.

He kisses her cheek gently and puts an arm about her as the voices and noises increase. They jump back and SISSI screams as the door is pushed in and CAPTAIN VON EBERHARDT is pitched into the room. He straightens up, shaking and brushing off the snow. He stands to attention.

EBERHARDT

Sorry about that, Sire. Your Serene Highness.

He bows before SISSI.

EBERHARDT

We've dug a way out for you.

He beckons for SISSI to precede him but she draws back.

LUDWIG

I'll go first. Come when I call.

He goes off, followed by CAPTAIN VON EBERHARDT.

SISSI steps forward, anxious.

SISSI

Your Majesty? Are you there, Your Majesty?

LUDWIG

(Offstage)

They've made a tunnel for us. So cold ... Sissi are you there? Sissi? Sissi! Where are you? Where are you?

SISSI makes to go forward, lifting her skirts over her arm. But she pauses, afraid.

LUDWIG

(Offstage)

Sissi?

She follows him off.

Fade to black.

ACT ONE SCENE THREE

The Mirror Room at Linderhof.

LUDWIG, exotically dressed in white flowing robes, with a white turban crested with a feather and a large jewel, strides about impatiently. His patience running out, he crosses, and pulls an ornate bell pull. The sound of the BELL, distant. He lifts the voice tube.

LUDWIG

Where – is – my – dinner?

Crackling sounds from the voice tube. He holds it away from his ear irritably.

LUDWIG

Now ... now!

He throws the voice tube aside, walks up and down. A table rises up from the floor. It is lavishly appointed for dinner. Five places are set. LUDWIG holds out chairs for his imaginary guests to sit. Then he sits himself, at the head of the table, which is placed on the diagonal, with LUDWIG upstage. He walks around the table, displaying the food to his imaginary guests.

ACT ONE

                    LUDWIG

Your beloved Majesty, I am aware of the impertinence
of offering this poor display of Bavarian rusticity.
Madame de Pompadour, Madame de Maintenon, my
pleasure and honour and delight – yes, delight – to
see the exotic flowers of France at my simple table.
A rose for you, Madame, a fragrant lily, Madame,
with my admiration. Oh – and His Majesty allows me
to say – with love. As ever, cher Louis, the greatest
of spirits – you are the model for us all – pray accept
this set of diamond buttons – I believe they were
Charlemagne's. Madame de Maintenon – rubies?
Ca va. Oh, how kind. I am relieved and gratified to
please. Madame de Pompadour – sapphires – I have
had them set à la mode, but if they do not please, we
shall submit to your commands with pleasure and
joy. *(He sits.)* You may find the eggs interesting. A
little Italian notion.

He helps himself liberally to food and begins to scoff. He helps
himself to drink – eats, head down, making low humming noises
of pleasure. The sudden whine of the voice tube startles him and he
jumps to his feet. He crosses, and picks up the tube.

                    LUDWIG
                    (Snarls)

What? Who? Who?? Ah. Ahh! Oh. But – yes, yes, yes,
yes, yes. And you – stay at the bottom of the staircase.
I don't want to see your face. No faces!

He wipes food from his mouth, throws off the turban and the
Arabian robe, tidies his hair in the glass. Satisfied, he turns and
waits. SISSI enters. They fly to each other and embrace. He lifts her
off her feet, twirling her round.

LUDWIG

But how? Why?

SISSI

You're here!

LUDWIG

Of course. Safe at Linderhof, my castle of dreams!

SISSI

No.

LUDWIG

No?

SISSI

You are not safe.

Pause.

LUDWIG

This is why you are here?

SISSI

Yes.

LUDWIG

To warn me.

SISSI

Yes.

He takes her coat. She collapses onto a seat.

SISSI

Forgive me – the journey.

He fetches her a crystal tumbler of water.

SISSI

Thank you. I came from Vienna.

ACT ONE

She drinks.

LUDWIG

Vienna? From Vienna? I thought you were in Switzerland.

SISSI

I had to go home for the Emperor's birthday.

She puts out a hand and strokes his face as he kneels beside her.

Pause.

SISSI

Ludo, I did a wicked thing.

LUDWIG

(He shakes his head.)

Impossible.

SISSI

I am a traitor to my country.

LUDWIG

Good. Excellent. What have you done? Raided the vaults for me?

SISSI

I went to the Chancellery – in an irresistible ensemble. And an even more irresistible hat. I had a pretty little box, silver, with emeralds. My begging box. For Austrian widows and children. I knew that the Chancellor and Herr von Brün were at the lake, fishing with my husband. It was one of those quiet days.

LUDWIG

So?

SISSI

I thanked them all for their wonderful generosity, looked into every face with love. And said that I was tired. That I would rest on the Chancellor's fine couch, and not to disturb me.

LUDWIG

(Slight pause)

And you were not disturbed?

She shakes her head.

SISSI

Of course not. I opened all the boxes. With my husband's key. So many! My poor eyes!

LUDWIG

You read the dispatches? Weren't they in code?

SISSI

Not the ones on Bavaria.

LUDWIG

Hah! What did they say?

SISSI

That you are to be – to be removed.

LUDWIG

Removed?

SISSI

Deposed.

Despite himself LUDWIG reels. He staggers to a seat and sits down, shaking visibly.

LUDWIG

You came.

ACT ONE

SISSI

Of course. I didn't dare to trust a messenger.

LUDWIG

No, no, no, no, no. No, of course not. *(A plea for help)* Sissi? Sissi ...

SISSI

Dearest?

LUDWIG

What am I to do?

SISSI

Survive.

LUDWIG

How?

SISSI

By moving swiftly. By removing every treacherous, lying traitor from your household, from your army and from your parliament.

LUDWIG

And how is that to be done?

SISSI

Call out the guard! Have them all arrested! Put a wall of steel around you. Protect yourself!

Silence.

SISSI

Is there no one – no one you can trust? There must be someone on your side.

LUDWIG

Architects – painters – composers.

SISSI

There you are – the people! The people are for you! You give so much work to so many of them. They'll defend you.

LUDWIG

With axes? Scythes? Against artillery? "Die Unruhe und Ungewissenheit sind unser teil." Unrest and uncertainty are our lot. What do they say, the dispatches?

SISSI

(Pause)

Instructions. For your incarceration.

LUDWIG

Incarceration? When? Where? How?

SISSI

Tomorrow. They intend to take you to Schloss Berg.

LUDWIG

That hideous … ? No, no, no, no, no, no, no, no, no. I see.

It's deliberate.

As SISSI makes to enquire.

LUDWIG

The place has bad memories for me. An old affaire. Go on.

SISSI

Preparations have been made to have you declared – declared …

She cannot go on.

ACT ONE

LUDWIG

Insane. Declared insane. Well, there is enough precedence for that in my family ... My brother, my aunt ... Go on.

SISSI

There is to be a formal announcement that you are no longer capable of performing your role – your position as King. The doctors will sign affidavits to that effect.

LUDWIG

Doctors? What doctors?

SISSI

Has no one – did no one approach – request to examine you?

LUDWIG

Do you think I would allow it?

Silence.

SISSI

(Quietly)

There is a list. Of what you've – or haven't ... What they think you ...

LUDWIG

(Snarls)

Nothing I don't know about.

SISSI

They have had spies placed round you.

LUDWIG

I should feel lost without them.

SISSI opens the leather folder and hands LUDWIG a sheaf of papers.

LUDWIG

I won't read this filth.

He throws papers into the air and paces.

LUDWIG

If they would just let me go quietly, with a pension.

SISSI

Has that been tabled?

LUDWIG

At my request – informally. I was advised, informally, that assassination would most certainly follow.

SISSI

They used that word – assassination?

LUDWIG

Vital for the stability of the realm, it seems. Why? Why?

He stoops, picks up the scattered papers.

LUDWIG

I'm sorry. Dearest one, how could I be so grotesquely ungrateful?

SISSI picks up the paper nearest to her, glances at it.

LUDWIG

What does it say?

SISSI

Such foolish, silly things.

LUDWIG

Go on.

ACT ONE

SISSI

Five different uniforms for your personal guard. Importing mango trees. The park for monkeys, parakeets and giraffes.

LUDWIG

The public loves my parks.

SISSI

They say they're silly.

LUDWIG

Go on.

SISSI

My dear, you know all this. Money spent on buildings, on operas, on rarities ... There's your hair ...

LUDWIG

My hair? What's wrong with it?

SISSI

They object to the way you carry an umbrella on parade.

LUDWIG

But it would go out of curl!

SISSI

They don't see it that way.

LUDWIG

I do everything to make them look splendid! Have you ever seen a soldier refuse new regimentals? I make them look beautiful.

SISSI

(Lifts the papers)

Shall I go on?

LUDWIG

No. These are old insults. Nothing new.

Silence.

LUDWIG

Wo steht das geschrieben? Where is it written? How should money be spent? On weapons? Or on flowers?

SISSI

Oh, my dear ...

LUDWIG

Which does the less harm? A gun? Or a magnolia tree?
(Slight pause.) Am I entirely – utterly foolish ... ?

SISSI

No. Not at all. As a woman, I must respect the imperative – the absolute and ultimate necessity for gentleness. I have carried a living human being, here, under my heart – felt the heart of another beating within me – the heart of my son. Not support what you stand for – the abnegation of force? I worship you for it.

LUDWIG

Oh Sissi – no, no. There's nothing admirable. My reasons are not moral or virtuous. I am against violence because, from whichever angle I peruse it, I can't – see – the – point!

SISSI

Oh, there's point enough.

LUDWIG

In real politik? What does it mean – real politik? Murder?

ACT ONE

SISSI

It means acquisition.

LUDWIG

To what end?

SISSI

To subjugate people, countries.

LUDWIG

Why? Must everything be swallowed into one maw?! Rule by force? Like Napoleon?

SISSI

Nothing more effective. Beat an animal and you have an obedient animal.

LUDWIG

(TIRED)

No. You have half an animal.

He sits.

LUDWIG

(Quietly)

Why not my way? Why not, Sissi? Why not music? Why not painting? Why not vibrant, honest, thrilling, absorbing life? Why not?

SISSI

Oh, my dear. One day.

LUDWIG

No. Not one day! Now! Why must they torture me? Tell me! I am not a failure!

SISSI

No, you are not!

LUDWIG

"Hatte Gott mich anders gewollt, so hätt'er mich anders gemacht." If God had wanted me different He would have made me so. Wouldn't he? How can you be a failure as an apple when you are an orange? Garibaldi's right. They offered him the crown of Italy – he said: "Don't be medieval. I am a sane man, ergo a Republican."

SISSI

(Thoughtful)

A Republic?

LUDWIG

Mmm?

SISSI

Ludo, if you abdicated and pronounced Bavaria a republic, would the people be happier – do better?

LUDWIG

Who knows? Reform offers promise. Sometimes it works. More often a mere change of hats.

SISSI

Oh, if I could understand any of it!

LUDWIG

I do what I can, to the best of my abilities – I use my energy, imagination, the money at my disposal - all, all for the people ... and I'm called mad for it.

SISSI

Then why not a Republic? If regality is medieval then a republic is at least au courant – de nos jours. The Socialists say ...

ACT ONE

LUDWIG

Oh, the Socialists!

SISSI

Do they alarm you?

LUDWIG

Mere theorists! What do they know?

SISSI

For a start, they say that God is not love, but justice.

Pause.

LUDWIG

Justice? Hmm. Even if they are right – which I beg leave to doubt, justice being the lesser quality – I know where I'll put my trust.

SISSI

In love.

LUDWIG

In love. And even if what they say is true, and justice is the source of all good, dearest heart, who am I to sit on my fatuous, badly designed and un-chosen throne and judge anyone?

SISSI

Surely we play the cards dealt, the game laid out for us.

LUDWIG

No! No, no, no, no, no. If the rules of the game make no sense … It must make sense! If nothing makes sense, Sissi, if everything is some fearful cosmic joke – some chaotic malevolence.

SISSI

It isn't. Remember when we were young and we were in the garden and you showed me a leaf?

LUDWIG

An oak leaf – a Spanish oak –

SISSI

And you said: "Look at this, Sissi – this has been designed." Not too rigidly, you said. You said that God was flexible.

LUDWIG

And you didn't know what flexible meant.

SISSI

I suspect that Satan doesn't.

LUDWIG

You're probably right. All straight lines.

Silence.

SISSI

Ludo, I'm afraid.

He takes her hand.

SISSI

Let me speak to the Emperor. I have his ear. He listens to me.

LUDWIG

As his ornament. We are not in the same position. I am a man. A King. With a country. An army.

SISSI

(Bewildered)

So, you DO want to lead your troops?

ACT ONE

LUDWIG

Yes!

SISSI

Into battle?

LUDWIG

Of course not! What are you talking about? Into life! Into literature, art, philosophy – Plato, Aristotle – Goethe – Schiller – Shakespeare!

SISSI

But beloved – with no army – who will protect us from the monsters? You know they exist. Those who must have what is yours because it is not theirs. There are times when we have no alternative but to fight. For survival – to protect our homes, those we love. Ludo, you must fight! For your life!

LUDWIG

Oh, my life ...

SISSI

Your people then. You say you love them ...

LUDWIG

Ah, but you see, they are not my people. Not yours, not mine – not theirs.

He jerks his head towards the door.

LUDWIG

They are their own people. I won't have it any other way.

SISSI

Then you are lost.

He picks up a paper, scans it.

LUDWIG

I see the Prussian Embassy gives the outrage its full support. Naturally. To be expected. En ce cas la – one solution. The only solution. Escape.

SISSI

Yes, Ludo, yes! Now – tonight!

LUDWIG

Oh, dearest! Darling girl. If only. This minute, fly away like swallows! Find an island, with sweet, mild air...

SISSI

Yes, but we must...

LUDWIG

Incense palms, hibiscus flowers for your hair...

SISSI

Now! We must go now!

LUDWIG

I haven't asked, how are the roses?

SISSI

What?

LUDWIG

Your roses. How is the Gloire de Dijon this year?

SISSI

Magnificent.

LUDWIG

And my Malmaison?

SISSI

Flowering wonderfully.

ACT ONE

But he walks away abruptly.

SISSI

Should we not -?

LUDWIG

(Turns)

Winter flowers are the best. Witch hazel – Wintersweet –snowdrops in the snow. Spring, of course. Autumn. *(Suddenly savage.)* Not summer! There is something wrong with summer.

Silence.

SISSI

Ludo – Ludo – I've come so far to see you. May I not persuade you?

LUDWIG

To put up a fight? How?

SISSI

It may be possible. There may be a way ... a plan could be arranged.

LUDWIG

A plan?

He laughs.

SISSI

Yes.

LUDWIG

How? Who can help me?

SISSI

Fritz.

LUDWIG

Fritz? You mean my Fritz?

SISSI

I sent for him. He forewent military duties to bring me here.

LUDWIG

Where is he now?

SISSI

Below.

LUDWIG rises, crosses to the voice tube.

LUDWIG

Hullo? Hullo? Hullo? *(Loud and angry)* Hullo! *(Jerks at the voice at the other end.)* What the devil do you think you're doing? Send up Captain von Eberhardt. Up here - Now! What do you mean, who? Von Eberhardt!

SISSI

You will listen to him?

LUDWIG

Why should he help? I threw him over years ago.

SISSI

He loves you.

LUDWIG

I wonder.

SISSI

He loves you! Why would he have cut manoeuvres, upset his General ...

ACT ONE

LUDWIG

All right. We'll see what he has to say.

They wait. A pause. They look at each other. Then there is a knock.

LUDWIG

Enter.

FRITZ enters. He bows to SISSI.

SISSI

Colonel Von Eberhardt.

LUDWIG

Captain – he's a Captain.

SISSI

Oh but -?

EBERHARDT

I – ah – I have had the honour to be promoted, Sire.

LUDWIG

No, you haven't. I haven't promoted you. Colonel?
Who says you're a Colonel?

EBERHARDT

General Obrecht, Sire.

LUDWIG

That ponce. Tell him he's fired. For insolence. Take a message.

SISSI

The General is here. We saw him on the steps.

LUDWIG

Clear off. Tell him I want to see him.

Silence.

LUDWIG

What's the matter? Have you gone deaf?

EBERHARDT

He – he's just left. This minute. On his way back to Munich.

LUDWIG

So, who's in charge below?

EBERHARDT

I am.

LUDWIG

You? You? Are in charge of me?

He makes to strike EBERHARDT

SISSI

Ludo!

LUDWIG

They've made you a Colonel – I see – I see – no, no, no, no, no, no, no, no, no. This won't do at all.

SISSI

Perhaps the Colonel – as your friend ...

LUDWIG

As my ex-friend.

EBERHARDT

Whose fault is that?

LUDWIG

You laughed at me!

EBERHARDT

So did the whole of Switzerland! Twenty alpenhorns! *(To SISSI)* One on every crag! Then they must all be

ACT ONE

put aboard a boat, for a river cruise. That was too
much, even for you.

LUDWIG

You never had a musical bone in your body.

EBERHARDT

When the Duke of Wellington and Prince von Thurn
und Taxis turned you down for loans, you ordered us
to rob banks.

LUDWIG

I had no money!

EBERHARDT

They think you're mad, Ludo.

LUDWIG

Be good enough to address me correctly.

EBERHARDT

I beg your pardon. Sire.

LUDWIG

If there was anyone whose loyalty I would have ...

Silence.

LUDWIG

What are your orders?

EBERHARDT

To convey you to Schloss Berg.

LUDWIG

(Waves a paper at him)
Where all the door handles have been removed and
peepholes driven through every wall!

EBERHARDT looks at SISSI, realizing where the information has come from.

> **LUDWIG**
>
> When is this – excursion – to take place, if we may be so bold as to ask?

> **EBERHARDT**
>
> Tomorrow morning.

> **LUDWIG**
>
> Tomorrow morning? Tomorrow morning? Get out of my sight!

EBERHARDT hesitates, agonized. He turns to go.

> **LUDWIG**
>
> You are a traitor to your country and to your King.

EBERHARDT stops, his back rigid. Then he exits.

> **LUDWIG**
>
> Sissi – quick! You must get me some poison.

> **SISSI**
>
> Poison?

> **LUDWIG**
>
> Yes, yes, yes. Some poison. I must have some poison! Do you really think I will allow them to take me there – to Schloss Berg! Hateful! Poison. *(Clicks his fingers.)* Poison.

> **SISSI**
>
> But dearest – how?

> **LUDWIG**
>
> There must be some below.

ACT ONE

SISSI

What shall I ask for?

LUDWIG

Don't ask – take.

SISSI

I don't know what it looks like.

LUDWIG

Oh my darling – forgive me. My only friend, and, as ever, I make your life even more impossible.

She holds out a hand. He crosses and sits beside her. His head sinks onto her shoulder and she kisses his hair.

LUDWIG

(Murmurs)

Palms. Casuarinas in the breeze. Beaches with fine soft sand ...

But he rises abruptly and begins to pace. He stops, gazes down at her. Then he resumes pacing.

LUDWIG

(Mutters)

It will be dark soon.

SISSI

Yes.

He paces. She waits, hands clasped in tension. He begins to stride more and more quickly until he is tearing manically round the room. She watches him, alarmed. And jerks back as he suddenly stops abruptly before her.

LUDWIG

Yes. Yes, yes, yes, yes, yes, yes, yes. Yes. *(He looks about him.)* I shall need a coat.

SISSI

A coat?

LUDWIG

A coat – yes, a coat! To take a walk!

SISSI

A walk? But ...

He takes her hands, lifts her to her feet and gazes into her eyes.

LUDWIG

Dearest friend. Belovéd. We'll endure. We will. We will endure. Believe me. Say you believe me. Say it.

SISSI

I believe you.

LUDWIG

I can't do it without you.

SISSI

I'm here.

LUDWIG

Not without your blessing. I need your blessing.

A long pause.

SISSI

No, Ludo. Don't. Don't ask that. Don't take away the only thing I have. You're all I have!

LUDWIG

Rubbish, you have your son. And Peko!

He shakes her arms to make her smile.

SISSI

No, Ludo. No.

ACT ONE

LUDWIG

I need you. I need your – your –

Silence.

LUDWIG

(Savage)

I do not want a military funeral. See to it.

SISSI

How am I to -?

LUDWIG

Get your stinking husband to wield his stick.
Remember everything – our games – our hopes – our dreams ... dressing up ... playing Hansel and Gretel.

SISSI

Please, Ludo.

LUDWIG

I must have your permission. You do see that, don't you?

SISSI

But what of me? I shall be alone.

LUDWIG

And haunted if you don't do as I ask. I ask it, Sissi. As your friend. Be mine. Please.

A silence. She stands before him, head bent.

LUDWIG

(Low)

Please.

Silence. At last she looks up into his eyes. She leans forward and kisses him gently on the lips.

LUDWIG

Good. Tell them.

He exits. SISSI goes to the other door. ERHARDT enters.

SISSI

His Majesty would like to take a walk.

EBERHARDT

A walk?

SISSI

Yes.

EBERHARDT

Now, Serene Highness?

SISSI

Yes.

EBERHARDT

It will be dark soon.

SISSI

Yes. *(Pause.)* I sent for you as his friend, Colonel. Why did you come? To assist in his destruction?

EBERHARDT

I was ordered.

SISSI

And you agreed.

EBERHARDT

I believed, Highness, that your presence ...

SISSI

Would save him?

EBERHARDT

No. It's impossible. Too late.

ACT ONE

SISSI

Then why? Why am I here?

EBERHARDT

To console him.

Pause.

SISSI

Do you think he's mad?

EBERHARDT

He's – unusual.

SISSI

It's not madness, it's ... If only you'd let him! *(She stops short, giving up.)*

Silence.

EBERHARDT

I'll arrange for an escort.

SISSI

Please don't.

EBERHARDT

Simply for his protection.

SISSI

From whom?

EBERHARDT

I'll escort him myself.

SISSI

I doubt if he'll have that.

LUDWIG enters, in a light coat. He carries a hat and a walking stick.

EBERHARDT

May I walk with you?

LUDWIG

Out of the question.

EBERHARDT

Merely as protection.

LUDWIG

Shut up. Is the doctor below?

EBERHARDT

Yes. *(LUDWIG glares at him.)* Yes, Sire.

LUDWIG

He can accompany me. For protection.

SISSI

I'll come with you.

LUDWIG

No.

SISSI waves at VON EBERHARDT to leave. He bows and goes.

SISSI and LUDO look at each other for a long moment.

LUDWIG

The basque suits you.

He nods civilly. And goes. SISSI restrains herself from running after him, from screaming. She lurches, almost falls, and collapses into a seat. And sits, immobile as a statue. A long, long, pause. She jumps as EBERHARDT enters carrying a silver tray with a flagon of wine. He pours a glass for her, leaves it at her elbow, bows and goes quietly. A long, long pause. SISSI sits, immobile. The candles burn low. And lower. EBERHARDT enters quietly. SISSI looks up in the gloom.

ACT ONE

EBERHARDT

Serene Highness ...

SISSI

His Majesty?

EBERHARDT

They have not yet returned.

SISSI

They?

EBERHARDT

The doctor accompanied him on his walk.

SISSI

(Murmurs)

Oh yes.

EBERHARDT

We have sent out scouts. I myself walked around the lake twice but ...

He is shaking slightly.

SISSI

Please, Colonel.

She indicates for him to sit. They sit in silence.

EBERHARDT

(At last)

I would have died for him.

SISSI

(Quietly)

Then why not save him!

EBERHARDT

No. Hopeless. He'll take nothing from me.

                    SISSI

Why not?

                    EBERHARDT

Because he treated me badly. I was abandoned.

                    SISSI

There must have been a reason for it. What was it?
Disloyalty?

                    EBERHARDT

No, something much worse. I bored him.

                    SISSI
                    (Rises)

Go and look! Search for him!

                    EBERHARDT
                    (Rises)

No, Ma'am. You are the empress of Austria. I must
stay here and protect you.

She sits and indicates him to sit. They sit in silence. He moves, restless. She waves a hand for him to take a drink.

                    EBERHARDT

Thank you.

He indicates the wine but she shakes her head. He drinks gratefully, refills the glass and drinks. Silence once more.

SISSI is as still as a statue. EBERHARDT fidgets, makes to take another drink, thinks better of it, sits back. Changes his mind and drinks again quietly.

The lights are now low. A feeling of peace, somnolence. EBERHARDT relaxes. The peace is broken by the sound of hoarse shouting offstage. EBERHARDT rises and leaves swiftly, his hand on the holster of his gun. SISSI remains seated and unmoving.

ACT ONE

More shouts, MEN'S VOICES.

EBERHARDT enters. SISSI looks up. A pause.

SISSI

What?

EBERHARDT

Dead. Drowned.

SISSI looks up, seeming vague, unable to take it in. She shakes her head. Then pulls herself together.

SISSI

The doctor?

EBERHARDT

Drowned also.

SISSI

How?!

EBERHARDT

They don't know. We don't know. They think ... They don't know.

Broken, he turns away.

EBERHARDT

No witnesses.

Pause.

SISSI

Have the bodies been recovered?

He turns to her, nods. She rises stiffly. He approaches to assist her. She looks up into his face.

SISSI

(Quietly)

May I see him?

He nods, unable to speak.

SISSI

Is he -?

EBERHARDT

There is no ... discoloration. He looks ...

His voice breaks.

EBERHARDT

... beautiful.

SISSI smiles gently, nods. She pauses, then lifts her head and leaves the room.

EBERHARDT follows her.

Fade to black.

THE END.

PALMAM QUI MERUIT FERAT

THIS BUST OF LORD NELSON EXECUTED IN MARBLE BY THE HON.ᵇˡᵉ ANNE SEYMOUR DAMER
ON HIS RETURN TO ENGLAND AFTER THE BATTLE OF THE NILE 1801 WAS PRESENTED BY HER
TO THE CITY OF LONDON AND IS NOW PLACED IN THE COUNCIL CHAMBER GUILDHALL

NELSON

For Patrick Sandford

NELSON

NELSON was first performed between the 26th October and 5th November, 2005, at The Nuffield Theatre, Southampton, UK.

CAST

Horatio Nelson	STEPHEN NOONAN
Emma Hamilton	CLAIRE FOX
Fanny Nisbet	HANNAH BARRIE
Cuthbert Collingwood	TOM BEARD
Hardy	NICHOLAS ASBURY
Sir William Hamilton	ROBERT MORGAN
Prince William	GRAHAM SEED
Queen of Naples	ALISON GARLAND
Tom (an old sailor)	GRANVILLE SAXTON
King of Naples/Jervis/Trowbridge	IAIN STUART ROBERTSON
Sailors of various ranks	STEVEN BEWS
	BRUCE HUNT
	JOHN RICHARDS
	DAVID PIERCE
Horatia	IMOGEN BAKER/
	SALLY BRITTON

The production used a community chorus of boy sailors and officers: JOSIAN HERSON, THOMAS LEOST, EDMOND SMITH and students from *Bitterne Park Secondary School* and *Woodlands Community School*.

Director	PATRICK SANDFORD
Designer	JULIET SHILLINGFORD
Lighting Designer	DAVID W KIDD
Composer	SIMON SLATER
Fight/Movement director	KATE WATERS

CAST

Sound Designer	DANIEL PAINE
Youth & Community Director	FRAN MORLEY
Casting Adviser	JOHN CANNON CDG
Stage Manager	GEORGINA RICHARDS
Company ManagerJ	ULIE BISCO
Wardrobe Mistress	ALY FIELDEN

The play was developed from a commission by Bath Theatre Royal.

FOR THE NUFFIELD THEATRE:
Artistic Director	PATRICK SANDFORD
Executive Director	KATE ANDERSON

NELSON

CHARACTERS

HORATIO NELSON
CUTHBERT COLLINGWOOD
PRINCE WILLIAM OF HANOVER
SPANISH ADMIRAL
LORD HOOD
SIR JOHN HERBERT
KING FERDINAND
CAPTAIN TROUBRIDGE
REVEREND NELSON
SIR WILLIAM HAMILTON
HARDY
CAPTAIN KINGSMILL
SPANISH CAPTAIN
TOM
BOSUN
EQUERRY
BATH RESIDENT #1
BATH RESIDENT #2
CHAMBERLAIN
SPANIARD #1
SPANIARD #2
BUTLER
MARINE CAPTAIN
COXSWAIN
SAM
SNOB #1
SNOB #2
SPANISH SHARPSHOOTER
FOOTMAN

CAST

TIMOTHY

SAILOR

DANIEL

COURTIER #1

COURTIER #2

WEDDING GUEST

GUEST #1

GUEST #2

JEM

HELMSMAN

WEDDING GUEST

SPANISH ASSASSIN

LADY EMMA HAMILTON

LADY HOTHAM

FANNY NELSON

QUEEN MARIE CAROLINA

HORATIA

MAID

ITALIAN MAID

COCKNEY MAID

PARLOURMAID

The play can be performed with ten men, three women, and two ASMs.

NELSON

ACT ONE

The stage, apart from the apron, is an impressionistic version of a three-masted 18th century square-rigged man o' war, with semi-practical sails, spars, braces, and halyards.

In the wings, large fans are sturdy enough to fill the sails.

There is a raised poop deck with a working hatch upon which is mounted the helm. Most of the stage is an approximation of the quarter-deck with – upstage – a number of cannons, cannonballs and gunpowder barrels along the bulwarks.

The quarter-deck contains an area which doubles as a domestic sitting-room and the captain's cabin.

The apron may be primarily used for the exterior scenes on land.

Also visible is part of the ship's stern, with its small square cabin windows, the name-plate of the vessel, and a British flag.

ACT ONE – SCENE ONE

Underway aboard 'Seahorse.'

Fade up on a spectacular night sky. A pin-spot picks out the name 'SEAHORSE' on the ship's stern. On the poop dock can be seen the shadowy figure of a HELMSMAN at the wheel.

HORATIO NELSON (18) and CUTHBERT COLLINGWOOD, rather posh (19), in midshipmen uniforms, are on deck, lying back on coiled ropes.

NELSON

What do you mean it's upside down?

COLLINGWOOD

It's the wrong way up.

NELSON

Where?

COLLINGWOOD

There! Orion!

NELSON

It can't be.

COLLINGWOOD

I tell you it's Orion – upside down!

NELSON rises and gazes at the sky.

NELSON

So it is. There's Rigel, the foot.

COLLINGWOOD

(Points)

And Betelgeuse, the armpit. And Aldebaran leading Orion down the sky.

NELSON turns and scans the heavens.

NELSON

God, the Milky Way looks lovely. *(Points)* Look, the Southern Cross.

He throws himself down by COLLINGWOOD. They gaze at the sky.

NELSON

A long way from the North Star ...

COLLINGWOOD

... and the Seven Sisters.

ACT ONE

COLLINGWOOD perches beside NELSON. Sounds of sails and rigging.

COLLINGWOOD

You have sisters, don't you Nelson?

NELSON

Yes. Three. And four brothers. There were eleven of us, but we lost three as squawkers.

The ship's bell rings twice.

COXSWAIN
(Offstage)

Let go and haul!

COXSWAIN and SAILOR appear in the background. Flapping sounds as they bring the foresails onto the wind again.

NELSON
(Growls)

Come on ... shorten!

COLLINGWOOOD

Pipe down.

He shoves NELSON back genially. They settle.

COLLINGWOOOD

What made you choose the sea?

NELSON

It was that or the Church.

COLLINGWOOD

Or politics.

NELSON

Politics! Not for me, what an insult. If ever I become a trimmer, you can sew me up and slide me down. No, the navy first and foremost. Why are you here?

COLLINGWOOD

My father's cousin is attached to the Admiralty.

NELSON

(Nods)

I have an uncle. Without influence you've no chance.

COLLINGWOOD

Oh, absolutely.

NELSON jumps up, and dashes offstage.

NELSON

(Offstage)

Wind backing nor'east a full point – lay off or come about!

NELSON re-enters.

Enter BOSUN – a fierce, seasoned seaman.

BOSUN

(Approaching)

Are you on watch, sir?

NELSON

(Mutters)

Bloody Bosun.

BOSUN exits.

COXSWAIN

(Offstage)

Stand by the braces!

NELSON, frustrated, paces. He stops, stares out to sea.

COLLINGWOOD

Awesome, isn't it?

NELSON dodges about, restless. Sounds of wind in the sheets.

ACT ONE

NELSON

(Yells)

Squall! She's backing! Lay off or come about for God's sake, helm!

The BOSUN enters and, as COLLINGWOOD rises, he knocks their heads together.

BOSUN

Get below or I'll have the pair of you flogged, braid or no braid!

They reel off.

The BOSUN exits. Sounds of the wind rising, sheets slapping, and a whine in the rigging.

BOSUN

(Offstage)

Avast! She's aback!

COXSWAIN

(Offstage)

Hard a-starboard!

Enter BOSUN.

BOSUN

Too late, she's aback! Stand by for sternway!

The HELSMAN struggles with the wheel. The deck seems to tilt.

Enter COXSWAIN, running.

COXSWAIN

(The Helmsman)

Larboard! Larboard your helm!

NELSON

              BOSUN
            (Bawls up at the riggers)
Let go – let go! If the port cannons shift we'll be
goners ... let go ... let go!!

Sounds rise to a screaming of wind, sheets, braces and sails. The sounds gradually die away, and we are left in darkness.

ACT ONE – SCENE TWO

A street in Portsmouth. Sound of seagulls. A bright, sunny day.

The corner of the ship's stern now resembles the corner of a tavern. A sign hangs over it saying: 'The Pompey Arms.'

              NELSON
            (Offstage)
It's the Admiral!

            COLLINGWOOD
            (Offstage)
Lord Hood!

ADMIRAL LORD HOOD, an elegant, patrician figure, accompanied by the bearded CAPTAIN KINGSMILL, enter, strolling and chatting.

A gust of wind blows off LORD HOOD's bicorne hat.

Enter NELSON, in lieutenant's uniform, and COLLINGWOOD, in lieutenant's uniform, from the tavern. They hurtle forward.

COLLINGWOOD gets the hat and makes to hand it to LORD HOOD with a bow – but NELSON puts a hand on his arm.

            NELSON
By your leave.

ACT ONE

He takes the hat from COLLINGWOOD, pulls out a large white handkerchief, wipes it reverently, bows, and proffers the hat to LORD HOOD.

LORD HOOD

Hmm. Young Nelson, ain't it?

NELSON

Yes, milord.

LORD HOOD

Out of ... ?

NELSON

Here in Portsmouth awaiting a ship, sir.

LORD HOOD

A ship! How old are you? I see you've got your buttons up.

NELSON

Twenty, sir.

LORD HOOD

Twenty, eh? And what would you do with a ship if you got a command, eh?

NELSON

I'd beat out to the West Indies after the renegade Yanks and their Froggie friends, sir.

LORD HOOD

And a few prizes, eh? *(He laughs)* What do you say, Kingsmill?

He confers with CAPTAIN KINGSMILL. They take their time.

> LORD HOOD

You of a mind? Good. *(To NELSON)* Well young Nelson, you're quick enough to dodge the grape shot. D'ye know the Albemarle?

> NELSON

Frigate, sir. Twenty-eight guns. None finer.

> LORD HOOD

She's yours. See what you can do for us.

LORD HOOD and CAPTAIN KINGSMILL continue on their way.

NELSON and COLLINGWOOD whoop with joy and head back to the tavern. The two older men glance back at them.

> CAPTAIN KINGSMILL

Very young for a lieutenant.

> LORD HOOD

His uncle's Captain Suckling.

> CAPTAIN KINGSMILL

Ah.

> LORD HOOD

Well, the navy looks after its own.

> CAPTAIN KINGSMILL

Absolutely.

They exit. Lights dim. Sound of a stiff ocean breeze.

Blackout.

ACT ONE – SCENE THREE

At sea. Day.

ACT ONE

Spotlight on name plate of vessel, which now reads: 'ALBEMARLE.'

Fade up stage-lights.

The sails bulge with wind. The HELMSMAN is at the wheel. BOSUN, COXSWAIN, and SAILOR are manning the braces.

NELSON, in a new Captain's uniform, paces the quarter-deck. Then he can't prevent himself hopping with happiness. He goes into a joyful dance – a sailor's jig – then throws his hat in the air and catches it.

The ship's bell sounds twice. NELSON stares up at the sails. Sounds of wind and sea increase.

Fade Out.

ACT ONE – SCENE FOUR

A Street in St. Nevis. Day.

Hot lights up on the apron – now furnished with a few palm trees. If there is a cyclorama, it shows the long curve of a tropical bay, fringed with beaches and vegetation. We are in the Caribbean.

TOM, an old salt – and Nelson's servant – is seated on a slab of white stone. With him are two boys: SAM and DANIEL

TOM is filling his pipe with tobacco from a leather pouch.

           TOM
What happens to you? What happens, lads, is you're doomed to live forever with live snakes for arms. That's what happens to them as falls foul of the 'orrible octopuses of the deep and their festering fangs.

The boys stop fidgeting and ponder this. TOM lights his pipe. SAM rallies.

> SAM
>
> You don't catch Sam there.

> DANIEL
>
> Me neither. Hey, what for the big ear-ring, mister?

> SAM
>
> Damn big feller, damn big ear-ring.

TOM clouts him over the head.

> TOM
>
> Less profanity, nipper, or I'll holystone that tongue o'yours.

> SAM
>
> Ow! *(Rubs his ear)*

TOM relents, and gives the boys a share of his tobacco. The three of them stoke up their clay pipes.

> TOM
>
> I'll tell thee what this is. *(He pulls on the large gold hoop in his right ear.)* You be looking at a Cape Horner.

They look up at him uncomprehendingly.

> TOM
>
> You never heard of Cape Horn? Cape Horn – the worstest and most treacherous seas in the whole wide world.

> SAM
>
> You seen it, mister?

ACT ONE

TOM

Seen it? I've ploughed it! Seen seas higher than the side of a mountain.

DANIEL

What's a mountain?

SAM

Big land stickin' up in the air. *(To TOM)* Higher than that?

He points to a palm tree.

TOM

Ten times as high.

The boys look at him scornfully and go.

TOM

Didn't believe it meself, lads.

Enter NELSON in Captain's uniform, with COLLINGWOOD in a lieutenant's uniform. TOM jumps to his feet and salutes informally.

TOM

Sir.

NELSON

Tom, I want you to take this over to Mrs. Nisbet and wait for an answer.

TOM salutes again, takes the letter.

TOM

Sir.

He exits.

NELSON

I ask myself Cuthbert ... will I ever be a married man?

COLLINGWOOD

Mrs. Nisbet's guardian still becalmed with the notion?

NELSON

More of a head wind. He thinks I'm after her money. *(At COLLINGWOOD'S glance)* Obviously, it helps. Talk of the devil.

SIR JOHN HERBERT, a thin, aging man, hoves into view.

NELSON

Good morning, sir. May I present Lieutenant Collingwood. His Excellency Sir John Herbert, Governor of St. Nevis.

COLLINGWOOD

A fine island you have here, sir.

NELSON

Mr Herbert is Mrs. Nisbet's guardian.

SIR JOHN HERBERT

And protector, sir. A widow with a young son to support A widow, moreover, with Prospects from one who loves her. Such a widow, sir, is in need of guidance.

COLLINGWOOD

Indeed.

SIR JOHN HERBERT

Marriage, sirs, is not a state to be entered into lightly.

COLLINGWOOD

Certainly not.

ACT ONE

SIR JOHN HERBERT

Where marital union is contemplated, there must be conformity. The law of contract requires a fair exchange.

COLLINGWOOD

A fair exchange – hmmph!

NELSON

And love?

SIR JOHN HERBERT

I beg your pardon?

NELSON

What of love? Where do you place love in your equation?

SIR JOHN HERBERT

Love, sir, is not a quantifiable commodity. It lacks rationale and moreover, in my experience of the world, has the characteristic of a Dwindling Asset. Not a sound basis for connection.

NELSON

My love for Mrs. Nisbet is based on esteem. A foundation, sir, on which passion may safely reside.

SIR JOHN HERBERT

So you say, sir.

NELSON

I take it that you look unfavourably on Fanny and me?

SIR JOHN HERBERT

Mrs. Nisbet has my advice.

NELSON

And that is?

SIR JOHN HERBERT

To wait.

Sounds of loud laughter. Enter HIS ROYAL HIGHNESS PRINCE WILLIAM, 30, expensively dressed in a feathered tricorne hat, pink silk frock coat, pearl satin waistcoat, pink silk breeches, white stockings and high-heeled buckled shoes. With him is his soberly dressed EQUERRY. NELSON and COLLINGWOOD bow.

NELSON

Your Royal Highness...

PRINCE WILLIAM

Nelson! By God, we meet in daylight – devilish bright, don't you know. Who's your friend?

NELSON

Lieutenant Collingwood, sir.

PRINCE WILLIAM

Collingwood, eh? Glad to know you, sir. Any friend of this lovely boy – what?

NELSON whispers in his ear.

PRINCE WILLIAM

Where were we, by God? *(To COLLINGWOOD)* So, you took ten guineas off me last night? Treason against the Crown! That must have been after I had that doxy against the wall. Weakens the brain. Who's the squirt?

NELSON
(Hastily)
Your Highness, may I present Sir John Herbert,

ACT ONE

> Governor of St. Nevis. *(To SIR JOHN HERBERT)* You have the honour of being presented to His Royal Highness, Prince William, beloved son of our Majesty, King George.

SIR JOHN HERBERT is overwhelmed. He bends the knee. Enter TOM, who listens in the background.

NELSON

Sir John, Sire, is guardian to my ... my special acquaintance, Mrs. Nisbet.

PRINCE WILLIAM

Your fancy? Is he, by God? How de do, sir. Up you get.

SIR JOHN HERBERT has trouble rising. PRINCE WILLIAM hoiks him up genially.

PRINCE WILLIAM

Well now, when's the wedding to be? I've a fancy to give the bride away. Suit you Nelson? *(To SIR JOHN HERBERT)* That suit, eh?

SIR JOHN HERBERT

(Stammers)

An honour – indeed an honour, Your Highness.

PRINCE WILLIAM

Good – splendid match. She won't do better than Nelson.
Only man in the Fleet who laughs at my jokes.

NELSON

Just keeping in, sir.

PRINCE WILLIAM yoks with laughter, and spars playfully with Nelson – almost knocking SIR JOHN HERBERT over. He rights SIR JOHN HERBERT roughly.

PRINCE WILLIAM

Off you go. We'll do it on Wednesday.

SIR JOHN HERBERT, trembling, bows and exits.

PRINCE WILLIAM

Well, Nelson, what do you say? We fixed you up, eh?

NELSON

(Dazed)

Your Highness ...

PRINCE WILLIAM

Wednesday, it is then! *(Goosing NELSON)* Got a decent uniform, have you? I'll send my tailor round.
Oh, ho ho!

He waves genially and goes, accompanied by his EQUERRY.

COLLINGWOOD

Does he mean it?

NELSON

I'm afraid he does. He remembers things when he's sober. What on earth is Fanny going to say? *(Calls)* Tom!

TOM steps forward.

NELSON

You delivered the letter?

TOM

Yessir.

NELSON

Mrs. Nisbet at home?

TOM

Yessir.

ACT ONE

NELSON hurries off.

TOM

So, it's to be the Captain and Mrs. Nisbet, sir?

COLLINGWOOD

So it would appear.

TOM

A lady with prospects.

COLLINGWOOD

Yes. Should go well.

TOM

(Sucks his teeth)

All the same either way for a mariner.

COLLINGWOOD

How do you mean?

TOM

Whichever way the wind blows, your sailor's absent most of the time, ain't he?

COLLINGWOOD

True.

TOM

(Slight pause)

A wifely sort of body, Mrs. Nisbet.

COLLINGWOOD

You disapprove of that?

TOM

No, not a bit, sir, but your wifely woman needs a warm bed, not a drawer full of letters and a man two oceans away.

COLLINGWOOD

The same for all sailors' wives, Tom.

TOM

Suits some more'n others, sir.

He salutes informally and goes.

COLLINGWOOD walks off thoughtfully.

Fade Out.

ACT ONE – SCENE FIVE

A blue sky. Flowering Trees.

Joyous church bells announce that the wedding is over. A MAID, 22, stands nervously, holding a tray of vol-au-vents. FANNY NELSON, 28, in a modest cream wedding dress, and NELSON, in a new hat and uniform, enter, arm in arm. They are followed by PRINCE WILLIAM, SIR JOHN HERBERT, COLLINGWOOD, EQUERRY, TOM – wearing a freshly-laundered stock – SAM and DANIEL in smart suits. The MAID offers her tray to PRINCE WILLIAM with a curtsey.

PRINCE WILLIAM

Ah – food for the royal chops, eh?

SIR JOHN HERBERT

(To COLLINGWOOD)

All these people! Who are they? What do they want?

COLLINGWOOD

To celebrate the wedding, sir. Honour your ward and Captain Nelson ... *(as SIR JOHN HERBERT turns away)* ... he's very well thought of, sir.

ACT ONE

SIR JOHN HERBERT

Yes, yes, yes, yes, yes.

He walks away. COLLINGWOOD follows him. FANNY NELSON is with the EQUERRY and DANIEL. NELSON is with TOM and SAM, who are being served by the MAID. NELSON leans down to talk to SAM.

SIR JOHN HERBERT
(To COLLINGWOOD)

My point is – why does he need to marry? She has everything she needs. All her wants are supplied. She has company – me – her boy, her aviary. Why does she need a husband? What can he provide that isn't already provided?

He walks off. PRINCE WILLIAM chases the MAID.

MAID

Sir – sir – please! *(She dodges away)*

PRINCE WILLIAM

I am a Prince, you know!

He lumbers after her, causing havoc.

COLLINGWOOD

Romantic soul, our Royal.

NELSON

Pity. Coming from a different berth he'd be a decent officer. *(He turns away, sees FANNY.)* Fanny!

She turns and comes to greet him. They smile into each other's eyes.

Lights down.

ACT ONE - SCENE SIX

A street in Bath – Day.

Projection of Georgian terraces on cyclorama. A sign announces: 'The Royal City of Bath, England.' RESIDENTS #1 and #2, in cloaks and hats, are taking their constitutional. An aristocratic woman, LADY HOTHAM (35) is strolling, chatting with SNOB #1 and SNOB #2. Enter FANNY and NELSON, arm-in-arm, and the REVEREND EDMUND NELSON (60), our hero's father.

The RESIDENTS doff their hats. NELSON notes that the snobbish group ignores them as they pass by. But then LADY HOTHAM turns.

LADY HOTHAM

Captain Nelson, isn't it?

NELSON

Ma'am. *(He bows)*

LADY HOTHAM

My husband is Rear-Admiral Sir William Hotham. No doubt you're acquainted with him.

NELSON

I've not had the honour, ma'am. A great pleasure to make your acquaintance.

LADY HOTHAM

(PERUSING HIM)

Ye-es. We saw you in London with Lord Hood. You're not afloat?

NELSON

Sadly not.

ACT ONE

FANNY

My husband becomes so restless ashore. Of course, we are pleased to have him with us.

LADY HOTHAM freezes her out. Turns to NELSON.

LADY HOTHAM

I'll have a word with the Admiral. See what we can do for you. Good day. *(She nods regally and sails off with her companions.)* Poor creature. A sailor without a ship is like a bird without wings.

NELSON is enraged. FANNY pulls him back.

NELSON

Hotham find something for me? Have you met him? Couldn't steer a bumboat out of Portsmouth harbour.

REVEREND

Oh, alas, preferment.

NELSON

Pa?

REVEREND

Preferment is like a hedgehog, full of spines and fleas.

FANNY and NELSON grin. He catches them at it and they all laugh.

NELSON

If they'd give me Something – anything! I write, I talk my head off, does anyone listen? I'm treated as a trouble-maker!

FANNY

Perhaps quieter steps? Obey first, query later – is that not the navy's rule?

NELSON

Obey? Who? I've no orders, no course to lay, no line of pursuit. No, there is only one hope.

REVEREND

And what is that?

NELSON

War. We need a war.

FANNY

A war?

REVEREND

Dear Lord in Heaven. You can't seriously wish to see your country and its people threatened?

NELSON

They won't be.

REVEREND

How not, if we're at war?

NELSON

They'll have ME!

Lights down.

ACT ONE – SCENE SEVEN

The Nelson Sitting Room – Day

FANNY is working on her pressed flowers. The REVEREND is relaxed in an armchair, reading. NELSON is at his table, writing a letter, a pile of newly-written letters at his elbow. He puts down his pen, seals his last letter, and adds it to the pile. The REVEREND smiles across at him.

ACT ONE

>   NELSON
>
> More of the same. To be disregarded.
>
>   REVEREND
>
> Lord Hood?
>
>   NELSON
>   *(Holds up top letter)*
>
> Three pages, begging for a cockleboat – a canoe ...

He crosses to FANNY, looks over her shoulder.

>   NELSON
>
> Pressed leaves?
>
>   FANNY
>
> Yes. Beech ... sycamore ... oak ... *(She turns the pages.)*
>
>   NELSON
>
> Ah – oak!

The REVEREND exits.

>   NELSON
>   *(Turning a page)*
>
> Flowers?
>
>   FANNY
>
> Daffodils ...
>
>   NELSON
>
> The petals – so delicate. How do you manage?
>
>   FANNY
>
> By being very gentle. *(They exchange a loving smile.)*

The REVEREND returns, holding a newspaper. He looks shocked.

>   NELSON
>
> What is it?

REVEREND

The unfortunate Louis is no more. He was beheaded yesterday in the Place de Louis Quinze ...

NELSON gets up and pulls on his jacket.

REVEREND

"He died with the most heroic fortitude. Last night a meeting of Cabinet Ministers was held at Mr Pitt's house in Downing Street, in consequence of which dispatches have been sent from the Admiralty and the War Office."

FANNY

Horatio?

NELSON

I must get to Old Nosy before any rivals.

He embraces her swiftly, bows to his father, and goes.

FANNY

Old Nosy?

REVEREND

Lord Hood.

FANNY

God help us all.

He puts an arm around her as she shakes.

Fade Out.

ACT ONE – SCENE EIGHT

The Captain's Cabin – Day

ACT ONE

Sounds of Battle. Cannon, musket and pistol fire. Men shouting. Explosions. Offstage, a battle is in progress. Pin-spot on ship's stern nameplate: 'AGAMEMNON.'

NELSON

(Offstage)

Helm a-starboard! Brace and shiver the driver and aftersails! *(Bawls)* Give her a broadside – through the stern windows – the stern windows, dammit!

Dreadful noise of a broadside.

NELSON

(Offstage)

Brace up the afteryards! Helm a-port!

HELMSMAN

(Offstage – calls)

Mizzen topmast away!

BOSUN

(Offstage)

Mizzen tops'l and crossjack yards away!

COXSWAIN

(Offstage)

She's yawing!

TOM

(Offstage)

Main mast's going, sir!

SAILOR

(Offstage)

Mast over, sir!

> NELSON
> *(Offstage)*
>
> Board her – board her! What? What?! Break off??

The sounds die away. NELSON enters the Captain's cabin, followed by LIEUTENANT COLLINGWOOD – both battle-stained and agitated.

NELSON'S left eye is now a glassy white.

> NELSON
> *(In a rage)*
>
> Break off?!!!

He throws himself into a seat at the table, glaring murderously.

> COLLINGWOOD
>
> I had to fly the order. What could I do? That was the signal!

> NELSON
>
> Ignore it!

COLLINGWOOD collapses into the seat across from NELSON.

> COLLINGWOOD
>
> You know the navy's rule.

> NELSON
>
> Yes, query later – from the seabed.

> COLLINGWOOD
>
> If every man decides for himself...

> NELSON
>
> It don't arise in battle! Battle is for Killing!

He pours himself a drink – and one for COLLINGWOOD.

> COLLINGWOOD
>
> Then why let a guilty man off a hanging?

ACT ONE

NELSON

He's a trained seaman. I need him.

COLLINGWOOD

You can't have insubordination in the confines of a ship. Fastest way to mutiny.

NELSON

You saw them out there. They fought like lions.

COLLINGWOOD

Because they worship you.

NELSON

So breed adoration. Become the idol of the fleet!

COLLINGWOOD

Can't follow you on that path.

NELSON

Make do with eccentricity, then. Sport a grey eye – at least they'll recognise you. We should have pursued them back to Toulon! Why hold back? Why? Now it's to be that fetid sink, Naples. To prop up a kingdom so weak it'll fall to the nearest flotilla of skiffs. Naples!

COLLINGWOOD

The orders stress diplomacy. The Queen of Naples is sister to Queen Marie-Antoinette of France – God rest her soul.

NELSON

And we need a refit.

COLLINGWOOD

Which we shall be able to achieve there. I'm told the British Ambassador keeps a fine table.

NELSON

(Still simmering)

We could have broken them! I need an Admiral's hat. If I'd commanded instead of Hotham, I'd have sunk the whole of the French fleet. Either that or seen red jam sluicing in the scuppers. I tell you, Cuth, it's unbearable.
(He rises) If I take ten sail and let one go, for me that is defeat.

He throws himself on his cot, lies back, groans.

COLLINGWOOD

What's the matter?

NELSON

My bloody eye aches.

COLLINGWOOD

Can you see out of it?

NELSON

Not a lot. *(He sits up)* Ugly, would you say?

COLLINGWOOD

No.

NELSON

They certainly look at me twice. *(Gloomily)* But that goes for all irregularity.

COLLINGWOOD

Not at all. You're handsomer than ever. They won't blench at the sight of you – take my word.

NELSON

Oh God ... the court of Naples. I'm not a lackey, I'm a sailor!

ACT ONE

COLLINGWOOD nods in agreement. They are both sunk in gloom.

Light change.

ACT ONE – SCENE NINE

The Court of Naples – Night

Baroque music.

A sign displays: 'THE COURT OF KING FERDINAND AND QUEEN MARIE CAROLINA OF NAPLES AND THE TWO SICILIES.' Upstage, on the deck, a velvet curtain now hangs from one of the spars. The COURT CHAMBERLAIN and COURTIERS #1 and #2 are standing informally, chatting to one another. They straighten up as ...

Enter KING FERDINAND, SIR WILLIAM HAMILTON (the British ambassador) – a spare man of discreet aspect, in his fifties – CAPTAIN NELSON, wearing an eye-patch, QUEEN CAROLINA, and LIEUTENANT COLLINGWOOD. KING FERDINAND, of Spanish origin, is heavily-built, not handsome. QUEEN MARIE CAROLINA, an Austrian, is, likewise, not well-favoured. Both have slight accents. The COURT CHAMBERLAIN fusses over the seating.

The KING shoves him aside and sits heavily. The others take their places.

> KING FERDINAND
> *(To NELSON)*
> Good boar-hunting here. You a shooting man?

> NELSON
> *(Drily)*
> From time to time, Sire.

KING FERDINAND

Good, good.

QUEEN MARIA CAROLINA leans across to NELSON.

QUEEN MARIA CAROLINA

We have this arranged in your honour, Nelson! *(She laughs like a young girl in anticipation.)* Sir William, we are now telling? No, for our so pretty Captain a surprise, I think.

SIR WILLIAM

Enchanting idea, Ma'am.

QUEEN MARIA CAROLINA
(To COLLINGWOOD)
Lady Hamilton is dearly beloved. Here we say ... What do we say?

SIR WILLIAM

Ma'am?

QUEEN MARIA CAROLINA

Sir William our fine English ambassador, darling Emma – sua Eccellenza L'Ambascatrice. *(Aside to NELSON)* We could not exist without the support of this creature and neither will you. Wait until you see her. Not so, Ferdinand?

KING FERDINAND

What?

QUEEN MARIA CAROLINA

Tonight! Our surprise – for the Captain!

KING FERDINAND

Yes, yes, yes. *(To NELSON)* Done any pig-sticking?

ACT ONE

The COURT CHAMBERLAIN raps his cane for quiet. COLLINGWOOD looks round, leans to NELSON in enquiry. SIR WILLIAM leans to COLLINGWOOD.

SIR WILLIAM
My wife is about to perform a tableau or two.

NELSON looks to COLLINGWOOD.

COLLINGWOOD
The Ambassador's wife is doing – I don't know.
Charades or something.

NELSON cringes. COLLINGWOOD shrugs in resigned apology. They sit back to endure the display. Whispering among the audience, then silence. KING FERDINAND falls asleep. Upstage, the ITALIAN MAID draws aside a velvet curtain to reveal EMMA HAMILTON – a beautiful woman of 28 – swathed delicately in gauze, as Venus from Botticelli's 'Birth of Venus.'

QUEEN MARIA CAROLINA
Ah, Botticelli!

EMMA smiles, nods civilly to the QUEEN, and retakes her pose. Murmurs and whispers of appreciation. The pose is discussed.

NELSON leans forward, gazes spellbound. SIR WILLIAM glances at him and smiles, pleased. The ITALIAN MAID draws the curtain. The QUEEN rises to applaud. The COURTIERS do likewise.

KING FERDINAND jolts awake, and then goes back to sleep again.

The audience anticipates the next tableau.

QUEEN MARIA CAROLINA
Now we are waiting for the very fine and moving
scene. For this – please – silence.

The COURT goes silent. NELSON leans forward. The ITALIAN MAID draws back the curtain. EMMA, nude, is displayed as the 'Virgin with Child' from the Bardi altarpiece.

Awed gasps. NELSON scrapes his chair as he turns away, and lowers his face. EMMA's head moves slightly to observe him. Then she is still again.

Lights down.

ACT ONE – SCENE TEN

Sound of calm sea swishing. A starry night.

The poop deck doubles as a balcony – decorated with flower-baskets. NELSON, alone, is looking out to sea. He has removed his eye-patch. His left eye gleams white and ghostly. He looks up, scans the sky, then turns at a sound. Enter EMMA.

> NELSON
>
> *(Bows politely)*
>
> Lady Hamilton.

A pause. They regard each other easily.

> EMMA
>
> Was I so very bad?

> NELSON
>
> Not at all. It went off very well.

> EMMA
>
> So why were you crying? You were weeping.

> NELSON
>
> *(Pause)* You made me feel lonely.

ACT ONE

> EMMA
>
> *(Thoughtfully)*

Lonely?

> NELSON
>
> Did they notice?

> EMMA
>
> Of course not. They were looking at me.

He laughs. Points up at the sky.

> NELSON
>
> Look. Your rivals.

She smiles. They gaze up. Then she looks at his upturned profile.

> EMMA
>
> Why are you lonely?

> NELSON
>
> I'm a mariner.

He turns and she studies his face. She touches his brow briefly over his bad eye.

> EMMA
>
> Hellish, your job.

> NELSON
>
> You think so?

> EMMA
>
> Confined in a wooden box – a lurching wooden box – a noisy, creaking wooden box – slaughter and destruction your only respite? Intolerable. I envy you.

> NELSON
>
> You envy me? Why?

EMMA

Because you can act. I can only ... act.

NELSON

You'd rather fight.

EMMA

But I am reduced, by accident of sex, to mere seduction.

She walks away, turns and surveys him.

NELSON

(Showing his profile)

Better by moonlight? Or worse? What are you thinking?

EMMA

I am thinking ... I am thinking – How can he be so brave and so slight?

NELSON

Does it put you off?

EMMA

That you are not a looming hulk? No fear.

They laugh. She returns to him and takes his arm. They look out to sea.

NELSON

Perhaps we should join the company?

She moves off and stops – turns and looks at him.

EMMA

I wonder. There's a grotto. I'll show you. It's made of shells and mother of pearl. If you have not had too much of the nautical.

ACT ONE

NELSON

I should like you to show me whatever pleases you.

Fade Out.

ACT ONE – SCENE ELEVEN

The Grotto. Night.

Light from the water outside flickers in waves across the iridescent, shelly interior. NELSON and EMMA are on the curved, decorated seat. The light picks out his face as, recumbent, he looks up at her, his face pale.

EMMA

(Murmurs)

How old were you when your mother died?

NELSON

I don't remember. Nine ... ten.

He puts up his arms, like a child, to be embraced. They remain – another tableau.

Fade Out.

ACT ONE – SCENE TWELVE

Seashore. Day.

Sound of the waves. Cyclorama: the Sea.

NELSON and EMMA are together on the shore, looking out across the waves.

> EMMA

Love me interestingly.

They embrace.

Sounds of the sea.

> *Fade Out.*

ACT ONE – SCENE THIRTEEN

Emma's Bedroom. Night.

Lit by candlelight.

NELSON and EMMA are lying naked on a bed.

He sits up, looks down at her.

> EMMA

Love me without pity.

Lights down.

ACT ONE – SCENE FOURTEEN

NELSON and EMMA are lying naked in bed.

> NELSON

I can't get enough of you. So much more to be pursued ... explored ... Emma ... Emma ... Emma. How and when do I reach the end of you?

> EMMA

Never, never, never, never, never!

NELSON throws himself on his back.

ACT ONE

NELSON

Thank God.

Lights down.

ACT ONE – SCENE FIFTEEN

Emma's bedroom. Day.

NELSON, with eye-patch, in his shirt sleeves, wearing an apron, is polishing Emma's shoes. He finishes the last pair, then tidies the long row. He puts the brushes away in a box. Enter EMMA in a negligee. She walks along the line, inspecting the boots and shoes. She points to one pair. NELSON removes her slippers, puts the shoes on her feet. She walks, turning to display them.

EMMA

Excellent.

NELSON removes one of her shoes, and kisses her foot.

EMMA

Very – good – work.

NELSON

(Holding her shoe)

Never allow these to be touched or breathed upon by non-naval personnel.

EMMA

And when the navy is at sea?

NELSON

Wear them caked in mud.

EMMA

Mmm. Dilemma. The British navy is always at sea.

(She bends and kisses him.) It seems I must wear mud on my shoes –

NELSON

– until I am ashore and can lick it off.

Enter SIR WILLIAM. He looks down at the row of shoes, puzzled.

SIR WILLIAM

Ah, shipshape and Bristol fashion! Dear hearts, forgive the intrusion.

NELSON

Signals?

SIR WILLIAM

I fear so.

NELSON and SIR WILLIAM leave quickly without a backward look. EMMA composes herself.

ACT ONE – SCENE SIXTEEN

On Deck. The Battle of Cape Vincent – Dawn

Sounds of battle. Loud cannon fire. Screams. Gunshots. Wind and waves. An explosion. The sound of a mast splintering and crashing.

Lights up on the poop deck. Billowing smoke. On the poop deck, NELSON is surveying the scene, a musket propped up beside him, and yelling orders. Behind him is an anxious COLLINGWOOD, pistol in hand. Behind them, the HELMSMAN is at the wheel.

NELSON

Cannoneers stop firing! Stop firing! Sergeant at arms! Ready your irons! *(Turns to Helmsman)* Into the wind – now! *(Calls to troops)* Stand by Marines!

ACT ONE

The HELMSMAN turns the wheels. A loud gunshot.

The HELMSMAN cries out and falls over the side with a splash.

NELSON

Cuthbert! Take the helm!

COLLINGWOOD does so – turning the wheel hard.

NELSON

Stand by Grapples! On my signal! *(NELSON raises his sabre.)* On my signal! Now! *(He sweeps his sabre down)*

A loud crash as the ship collides with another. An explosion.

COLLINGWOOD and TOM duck. NELSON doesn't flinch. More smoke. NELSON aims the musket high and fires.

A SPANISH SHARPSHOOTER falls, screaming, from the rigging and out of sight behind the upstage bulwarks. NELSON puts down the musket. Sound of bullets whizzing through the air. A bullet explodes on the bridge next to NELSON.

COLLINGWOOD

We should get below! This is too rash!

NELSON

What?

COLLINGWOOD

Too rash!

Enter TOM and SAILOR fighting with cutlasses and truncheons, SPANIARD #1 and a SPANISH CAPTAIN, who are armed with halberds and swords. A SPANISH ASSASSIN, a poniard in his teeth, climbs unobserved up on to the poop deck.

NELSON

Behind you!

COLLINGWOOD turns and shoots SPANISH ASSASSIN, who falls backwards off the deck, out of view.

> NELSON
> (Yells)
> Bring down the foresail! Down the foresail!

On the quarterdeck, SPANIARD #1 kills SAILOR. Enter SPANIARD #2 who attacks TOM.

> COLLINGWOOD
> For God's sake Horace – you are too exposed! You must get below! We need our commander!

> NELSON
> (To COLLINGWOOD)
> Steady as she goes.

NELSON, sabre in one hand, draw his pistol with the other. He leaps from the poop deck onto the quarter-deck where he shoots dead SPANIARD #1 at close range, then runs through SPANIARD #2 with his sabre. TOM sword-fights with the now retreating SPANISH CAPTAIN. A loud explosion. A huge spar falls with part of a torn, smoking sail.

Blackout.

ACT ONE – SCENE SEVENTEEN

On board ship – Day.

Sound of the sea. A brisk wind is dispersing the smoke.

On the quarter-deck is a table. COLLINGWOOD stands by stiffly. NELSON waits, bicorne hat and eye-patch on, adjusting his uniform. TOM stands behind him. Also on deck are the

ACT ONE

HELMSMAN, COXSWAIN and SAILOR, all laden with loot – halberds, fancy clothing, hats, Spanish swords and boots.

At the rail, the BOSUN plays a pipe – piping aboard two visitors.

Enter the SPANISH ADMIRAL and SPANISH CAPTAIN holding two swords, up the gangplank. The BOSUN picks up his musket and follows them. The SPANISH ADMIRAL steps up to the table. He and NELSON eyeball each other. Then the SPANISH ADMIRAL bends his head, takes the two swords from his CAPTAIN, and presents them formally to NELSON. NELSON doesn't know what to do with them. He turns and hands them to TOM – who slings them on the deck behind him. The SPANISH ADMIRAL and the SPANISH CAPTAIN are outraged.

> SPANISH ADMIRAL
> (In Spanish)
> In the name of the Virgin and all the Angels, this is beyond outrage!

NELSON looks at TOM, baffled. TOM shrugs. The SAILORS watch, gratified. NELSON nods to the BOSUN who hustles the furious Spaniards away. NELSON struts and raises his hat to his victorious crew. The SAILORS erupt in an explosion of incoherent cheering, waving their spoils above their heads.

Blackout.

END OF ACT ONE

ACT TWO

ACT TWO – SCENE ONE

Sir William Hamilton's sitting room – Day

Elegant furniture. A warm light coming through windows.

NELSON and SIR WILLIAM HAMILTON are seated. NELSON has lost his right arm. On a side table are bottles of medicine and a bowl containing a cold compress. A BUTLER pours drinks and leaves.

> NELSON
>
> Crossfire as we passed the mole.

> SIR WILLIAM
>
> Thank God you were so near, in reach of doctors to save your life. Much blood loss?

> NELSON
>
> Enough. The next time I lose an arm, the sodding surgeons can heat the knife first. A cold blade is the worst thing for flesh to tolerate.

> SIR WILLIAM
>
> A thought that makes you think.

> NELSON
>
> Aye.

> SIR WILLIAM
>
> Warm the cutlasses before boarding, eh?

NELSON smiles briefly.

> NELSON
>
> Look at me, William. I'm half a man.

ACT TWO

SIR WILLIAM

Not at all. Not in the vital area.

NELSON

But will she want me like this?

SIR WILLIAM

More than ever, I assure you.

NELSON

Well, you know her, but no doubt you're being diplomatic. Tell me the truth. I want no pain for her. Better that I should leave quietly. I'm not a pretty sight – the wound is still open ...

He shakes his head in misery.

SIR WILLIAM

Does it hurt?

NELSON

Shall I tell you the worst? My fingers, which are no longer there, throb. My disappeared wrist hurts, my absent elbow hurts. *I* hurt.

EMMA flies into the room.

EMMA

Oh, my beloved! My hero! Let me look at your dear face. Oh, you are more beautiful than ever. Pain has made you glorious. Oh William, we have our most precious treasure here under our roof. I shall nurse you and the pain will slip away and you will sleep like a boy and we shall create simple, lovely things for you to eat and make one-armed men the most fashionable creatures on the planet. First you must be well. Rest, sleep, and more rest.

NELSON

SIR WILLIAM slips discreetly away. EMMA makes NELSON comfy on the sofa, then puts a cold compress on his forehead.

> NELSON
>
> Am I running a fever?

> EMMA
>
> Very little.

She gives him a draft of medicine.

> EMMA
>
> Have you told Fanny of your wound?

> NELSON
>
> Not yet. She'll only fuss.

She bends over him. He kisses her lips gently.

> EMMA
>
> Think of sun and stars and idleness – and ships and what to do when you are recovered, and who to promote – who is worthy and who isn't and how to ...

> NELSON
>
> *(Sleepy)*
>
> How to win. *(Pause)* How is your tush?

EMMA smiles down at him.

> NELSON
>
> Good.

She sits, watching over him until he sleeps. Then she bends and kisses him, covers him with a light rug, and walks off quietly.

Fade Out.

ACT TWO

ACT TWO – SCENE TWO

Bedroom at Sir William's Embassy – Day

NELSON is on a daybed. TOM is helping him on with his shirt.

Enter LIEUTENANT HARDY – a good-looking officer, 28, with letters. TOM picks up a bowl and bandages and exits.

NELSON

Ah – Hardy.

HARDY

The French have broken out of harbour.

NELSON

(Sits up)

What? Bound where?

HARDY

We're awaiting a signal.

NELSON

What else?

HARDY

New orders. Gunnery practice every forenoon.

NELSON

Bloody army interference! The navy – poor marksmen? Bloody Arthur Wellesley should keep his mouth shut. How many battles has he won? Imagine fighting on solid ground! Where's the art in that?

He gestures to HARDY to read the mail to him. HARDY opens a letter.

HARDY

Their majesties are returned to Naples and are pleased to wait on you.

NELSON

(Murmurs)

Oh bugger.

HARDY opens another letter.

HARDY

You are offered the freedom of the city of Norwich.

NELSON

That'll please father as a Norwich man. *(As HARDY has his head down over another letter.)* Well?

HARDY

It's from Lady Hamilton, sir.

NELSON

Give it here. *(He tries to sit up but is too weak. He gestures for HARDY to read.)* Carry on.

HARDY, embarrassed, clears his throat.

HARDY

(Reads)

"Beloved – I hate to be away from you and would not – could not if the dear Queen were not so dependent on my friendship. But – dearest heart – we arrive in the morning. I shall come to you with dried manure in my hair from the carriage wheels, but I must see your beloved face." I must see your beloved face in capital letters, sir.

NELSON

When does she arrive?

ACT TWO

HARDY

Today, sir. *(Clears his throat)* There is more, but for your eyes only.

NELSON stretches for the letter, and clutches it. HARDY opens the last letter.

HARDY

Ah. From Lady Nelson.

NELSON nods for him to read.

HARDY

My dear Horatio. Still no word from you. Your poor father and I are suffering sleepless nights. However, there is news from Collingwood that you are on the mend. Did the boxes arrive? The plum jam is not so good this year, but have enclosed six pairs of stockings, your slippers and silk shirts. Do please send word. You have no idea of the worry we suffer. We await news that you are taking ship. Pray God it may be soon. As ever, your loving and faithful wife, Fanny. *(Silence.)* Right, sir.

He makes to leave.

NELSON

(In a rage)

No! Not right! Tell her she's sent the wrong slippers. The jam was so badly packed that it ruined the shirts, and will she be good enough to send twelve – repeat twelve – pairs of stockings as requested!

HARDY, embarrassed, leaves.

Lights down.

ACT TWO - SCENE THREE

The Court of Naples – Night

Courtly music. A formal dance is in progress. MALE GUESTS #1 and #2 dance a quadrille.

Enter KING FERDINAND and QUEEN MARIE CAROLINA, SIR WILLIAM HAMILTON, LADY EMMA HAMILTON, NELSON (with eye-patch in an Admiral's uniform) and LIEUTENANT HARDY. QUEEN CAROLINA, SIR WILLIAM HAMILTON, LADY EMMA HAMILTON and NELSON join the dance.

> QUEEN MARIE CAROLINA
> *(Circling NELSON in the dance)*
> Ah, my darling wounded sprite. Spare me one glance, won't you?

> NELSON
> I dare to dream, beloved majesty.

He breaks away, circles EMMA.

> EMMA
> She fancies you.

> NELSON
> She can't have me.

They dance.

> QUEEN CAROLINA
> *(As she and NELSON come together)*
> Adorable imp.

> NELSON
> Beware, madam – I am not tame.

ACT TWO

The QUEEN shrieks with delight. The dance ends. Enter ITALIAN MAID, who serves drinks.

QUEEN MARIE CAROLINA

I hear you will leave us now, Nelson.

NELSON

Duty calls, majesty.

KING FERDINAND

You are well enough in your health ... ?

NELSON

I'll do.

KING FERDINAND

Because the vile Frogs must be stopped.

NELSON

They will be, sire.

He stands alone, looking pale and ill.

QUEEN MARIE CAROLINA

You long to be on your boat, Nelson, yah?

NELSON

(Short laugh)

Ever been sea-sick, Ma'am?

QUEEN MARIE CAROLINA

Certainly not.

NELSON

Sea-sickness is no respecter of persons.

QUEEN MARIE CAROLINA

Surely not you?

NELSON
(*Nods*)

If I've been ashore long enough.

KING FERDINAND

You – the Admiral – are sick?

HARDY

Same for us all.

NELSON

Which is why we stay afloat. Never call the Frogs sailors, they are landsmen. You are safe because we are on guard, 24-hour watch – out there. At sea. Where we belong.

KING FERDINAND

Good. Good. Very good. Very good.

QUEEN MARIE CAROLINA

Poor Lady Hamilton will miss you.

EMMA

Nelson must be where Nelson is needed. You will hear no complaint from Sir William and me however much we miss him.

KING FERDINAND
(*Raising glass*)

To Nelson!

ALL

To Nelson!

NELSON is toasted. It pleases him. He lifts his fin (his right shoulder) in acknowledgement.

Lights down.

ACT TWO

ACT TWO – SCENE FOUR

Spotlight on the nameplate of the ship: 'VANGUARD.'

The Admiral's Cabin – Day

Sound of the sea. Present are ADMIRAL NELSON, CAPTAIN TROUBRIDGE, a seasoned officer, LIEUTENANT HARDY and a MARINE CAPTAIN (40). NELSON is perusing a report of enemy movements.

NELSON

Forty thousand troops, artillery, horses, cavalry, artificers, astronomers, mathematicians? Napoleon needs all this for the taking of Malta? Troubridge?

TROUBRIDGE

He'll be after bigger quarry than Malta, sir.

MARINE CAPTAIN

Corfu? Constantinople?

HARDY

Naples and Sicily are safe.

TROUBRIDGE

They'll be sailing west then – running downwind to join forces with the Spanish.

HARDY

By God, we'll be outgunned.

TROUBRIDGE

A fleet three times our size.

NELSON glares at him, then paces. They wait. NELSON stops abruptly.

NELSON

Astronomers? Mathematicians? Cavalry?

                    TROUBRIDGE

Obviously planning a land battle.

                    NELSON

So why ship them by sea to Spain?

TROUBRIDGE shrugs. He does not know.

                    TROUBRIDGE
                    (To HARDY)
With Napoleon, there'll be some devilish plot.

NELSON paces. They wait. He stops.

                    NELSON

He's sailing east.

                    HARDY

East?

                    NELSON

It's Egypt.

                    TROUBRIDGE

Egypt?

                    HARDY

Why?

                    TROUBRIDGE

What possible tactical advantage?

                    HARDY

The other end of the Med?

                    NELSON

If Napoleon controls Egypt, he controls the Red Sea.
From the Red Sea, he can be in India in three weeks.

They gawp at him, mystified.

ACT TWO

NELSON

India! The riches of the Orient, by God! *(He laughs at the audacity of it.)*

HARDY

Shipping an army to the Levant?

TROUBRIDGE

Not even Napoleon would hatch such an unlikely plan. What about supply routes?

NELSON

He's sailing east.

Silence.

HARDY

The complement of their fleet ... It could – just – make sense.

TROUBRIDGE

Unlikely.

MARINE CAPTAIN

Days before we know if we're on the right tack.

TROUBRIDGE

And to commit the fleet, with no signals, no evidence of movement ...

A murmur of assent.

HARDY

We need Collingwood's cool head.

TROUBRIDGE

Yes, reasonable man. Pity he's not aboard.

NELSON

Who?

TROUBRIDGE

Collingwood.

NELSON

Ah, Collingwood. As you say, a reasonable man. *(He hits the table with force.)* I am not a reasonable man!

HARDY

Good Lord, Admiral...

MARINE CAPTAIN

Not at all...

NELSON

And you know why? Because war is not reasonable. War is against reason. For war we must turn men into mechanisms for destruction. Into beasts. Fiendishness is what we inculcate. Decency has no place. Do I want a fair fight? *(As they nod.)* No! I want advantage. A fight as unfair, as one-sided as I can command. By any means. By all available device.

HARDY

Fair means or foul?

NELSON

Belay fair. It is not my disposition. A Collingwood is for fair. The rational. For returning chaos to order – madness to sanity.

TROUBRIDGE

Absolutely.

NELSON

A Nelson ... A Nelson is for destruction ... treachery ... Above all, for attack! Collingwood is a fine officer. He is my friend. And enemy. I will not

ACT TWO

have reasonable men about me. He is a reproach. Get
out the charts. We sail for Egypt.

He walks off.

MARINE CAPTAIN

By God, that was chilling.

TROUBRIDGE

Bloody outrageous. And he's wrong! We'll be in the
wrong place. Out of contention. Madness.

HARDY

(After a pause)

Egypt it is, then.

TROUBRIDGE

The little prick. God help us all.

They pore over the charts.

Lights down.

ACT TWO - SCENE FIVE

Sound of the sea.

On Deck. Night - Moonlight.

On deck are TOM and two young sailors, TIMOTHY and JEM.

TIMOTHY

Then what?

TOM

We covers our eyes like honest, God-fearing men and
stumbles through the swamp in our sea boots with
the giant sea snakes a-snapping and a-hissing great

gobs of ginger shit at our eyes. 'Keep your eyes down!' I shouts – but there's never been a mess deck yet not littered with a flavourin' o' fools.

JEM

They got some on 'em?

TOM pulls off his woollen sea cap in respectful remembrance, and shakes his head sadly.

TOM

Oh aye. Scuppered they was.

TIMOTHY

Killed?

TOM

Would they hadda been, lads. Oh no. Them that gets hissed in the eyes by the Giant Sea snakes of the Mouldering Swamp is doomed to live horribly ever after scaring the boots off all who falls afoul of them.

TIMOTHY

What happens if you sees one?

TOM

Your pizzle falls off.

Silence. The sounds of slatting sails, sheets and braces.

TOM

We're sailing free now. The wind's well abaft the beam.

JEM

Where we headed, Tom?

TOM

Back down to Alex. When we didn't find him there, Troubridge reckoned Boney had pissed off to Corfu.

ACT TWO

Sittin' on northerlies they could drop down anywhere
in the Med. But he was wrong. The Admiral was right.
Egypt. Only we got there too soon. Boney was slowed
up with his troopships.

JEM

Troops?

TOM

Aye. We're in for a fight, lads. Good sport, never fear,
you'll enjoy yourselves. All you has to do is remember
Rule Number One.

TIMOTHY

What's that?

TOM

When we boards, don't fall in.

JEM

All the same to me. I can't swim.

TOM

Good. You'll be drownded all the quicker. Happened to
a mate of mine. Haven't seen him since.

He makes a warning sound. NELSON appears on the quarterdeck.

TOM

Summat's up. His fin's twitching.

NELSON exits. A reverent silence.

TIMOTHY

The surgeon's mate's learning me to write so's I can
let 'em know in Deptford as I'm on board with Nelson.
Course they'll never believe me.

Four bells. They go. NELSON and TROUBRIDGE appear on deck.

TROUBRIDGE

We've lost them.

NELSON

They're in Alexandria.

TROUBRIDGE

If they are, they're safe in harbour under the batteries, and we're in for a blockade. Or they've disgorged their troops and are off.

NELSON

Then we'll catch them at sea.

Light change.

ACT TWO - SCENE SIX

On Deck – Day

Full sunlight. The HELMSMAN is at the wheel.

On the quarterdeck, TOM is leaning over the gunwhale, hand over his eyes, searching for the enemy. Also present are the BOSUN and the COXSWAIN. The SAILOR swings from the yard to a backstay, and slithers down to the deck, then hurtles across the stage to the COXSWAIN. The COXSWAIN hoists the signal: 'Enemy In Sight.'

BOSUN and SAILOR climb the rigging for a view of the French Fleet.

NELSON comes on deck, putting on his coat – TROUBRIDGE at his side. They look with telescopes.

TROUBRIDGE

By God, there they lie.

ACT TWO

NELSON

Like a covey of fat pheasants.

BOSUN

(Aloft, calls)

Thirteen sail of the line and a whacking lot of frigates and small craft!

HARDY joins them.

HARDY

By God, Admiral.

NELSON

Ah Hardy. Tomorrow I shall have gained a peerage or a slab in Westminster Abbey ... either will do.

NELSON leans over and calls to Lord Hood in the 'Zealous,' sailing close on his bow.

NELSON

Lord Hood sir! Can you take your ship round the end of the enemy line?

LORD HOOD

(Offstage. Calls from a distance.)

Can try but we don't know the lie of the shoals!

NELSON speaks to TOM.

TOM

(Calls)

Take soundings! Take soundings!

NELSON

(Calls to Hood)

Good luck Admiral! *(To Troubridge)* Hood's making sail.

TROUBRIDGE

God wish him well. What a sight. Thirteen great ships of the line. There goes Captain Foley in the Goliath.

The sun begins to set.

NELSON

He's overhauling the Admiral. By God! By God! *(He leaps up on to the gunwhale.)* Do you see? Foley's seen it! Foley's seen it! The French ships are only anchored by the bow. There must be room for them to swing 350 degrees clear of the shoals. There's water all round them! Where there's water for one 74 gun- ship to swing, there's room for another to sail past! Come in on an angle, blast the last in line from the rear and steer round the head of the line. Keep about six foot off our rigging and blast them on the blind side!

He dances up and down. Flashes of light, and sound of guns.

Blackout.

During the blackout, SOUNDS of a major sea-battle. Finishing with a massive explosion.

ACT TWO – SCENE SEVEN

The Admiral's Cabin – Night.

NELSON, battle-weary, his head bandaged, is dictating to HARDY. TOM and the COXSWAIN stand by.

NELSON

To your Majesty and your Lordship. Almighty God has blessed His Majesty's Arms in the late Battle by a great Victory over the fleet of the enemy, whom I

ACT TWO

attacked at sunset on the 1st of August, off the mouth
of the Nile. I estimate French losses as six times those
of our fleet at 1700 killed, 1500 wounded, and 3000
taken prisoner. Of the seven ships taken, six are fit to
be commissioned into the Royal Navy. To single out
individuals would be invidious. The judgement of the
captains, together with their valour and that of their
officers and men of every description, was absolutely
irresistible. Could anything from my pen add to
the character of the captains, I could write it with
pleasure, but that is impossible.

He faints, and is carried to his bunk by TOM and the COXSWAIN –
his shoe falling off.

Fade to black.

ACT TWO – SCENE EIGHT

A Bathroom – in Naples – Day

NELSON is in a bath. The ITALIAN MAID brings large copper jugs
of water, tops up his bath, and leaves.

EMMA enters and washes his hair, then rinses it from a smaller
jug. Then she washes him like a child. She helps him out of the bath,
enfolding him in a large towelled dressing gown, so that we are
spared the sight of his stump. EMMA dries him. NELSON watches
her. The sound of SHOUTING, offstage.

NELSON

What is it?

He hurries off. The sound of voices. EMMA waits anxiously.
NELSON reappears, followed by TOM.

NELSON

Emma. Pack everything of value. I have informed their Majesties and Sir William.

EMMA

What? Why?

NELSON

The French army have broken out and are already south of Rome. We sail for Sicily on the tide.

EMMA

Cannot we make a stand?

NELSON

With what? Militia?

EMMA

I'll go to the Queen.

She exits.

TOM

All right, sir?

NELSON

We've been out-flanked dammit! I look a fool! We must get the Royals to safety. How many ships has Sir William commandeered?

TOM

Not sure, sir, but there's a lot of vases and statues being loaded aboard!

NELSON

Oh Christ!

He exits quickly.

TOM starts packing – putting things together calmly.

ACT TWO

ACT TWO - SCENE NINE

Ship - In Port - Sicily - Dusk.

Sound of the sea.

A gangplank has been laid between the quarterdeck and the apron. Two bollards indicate the harbour strand. NELSON is ashore. The COXSWAIN and SAILOR are present at the stanchions as KING FERDINAND and QUEEN MARIE CAROLINA - in a vomit-drenched white dress - make their way shakily down the plank to the harbour, where they are helped off by NELSON. The QUEEN is in shock. They are followed by LADY EMMA HAMILTON and a queasy SIR WILLIAM HAMILTON.

EMMA
(To NELSON)

The Queen's youngest child died of convulsions in the night.

She crosses to a dazed QUEEN MARIE CAROLINA and helps her offstage. SIR WILLIAM helps the bewildered KING FERDINAND.

KING FERDINAND
(To NELSON)

I had not known the sea could be so rough.

KING FERDINAND and SIR WILLIAM exit.

The COXSWAIN and SAILOR exit. Enter EMMA.

NELSON

The Little Palace is prepared for them.

EMMA sits on a bollard, exhausted, hands on knees. NELSON offers her his hand, but she remains seated. The sound of the sea.

EMMA looks up.

EMMA

I say this, Nelson. If men grew arms and legs in their bellies, they would not be minded to dispose of them so lightly.

NELSON

And the alternative? Napoleon in Whitehall? Occupation by the French?

EMMA

Yes, rather than lose one hair of one baby's head.

NELSON

What if he came at you with a sword, to kill that baby?

EMMA

I'd shoot him. *(Her shoulders droop.)* I'm tired.

He looks down at her. Pause.

NELSON

I lusted after you from the moment I saw you. As most men, no doubt. Now I love you. I have seen you, through that storm, when we were like to founder, every man, woman and child on board sick with fear, infuse that ship with courage. You are an Amazon. You share not just your beauty but your sagacity, your hope. You make us all survive – you insist upon it. You are the bravest creature I know.

EMMA

No. Nelson is that.

NELSON

(Dismissive)

Oh, attack is simple.

ACT TWO

EMMA

Are you never afraid?

NELSON

No. I faint sometimes. And I often weep.

EMMA

Your secret is safe.

NELSON

Oh, they all know.

EMMA

What I know is this. My reason for being is to keep you alive. *(She rises)* How can an Emma exist without a Nelson? I would be dead in six months – three, two, a week. *(She takes his arm)* Air that is not breathed by Nelson will not be breathed by me.

They embrace fiercely, and go.

ACT TWO – SCENE TEN

Sitting Room – London – Day

An armchair, sofa and side-table. Nelson's wife, FANNY, 37, is sitting with the REVEREND EDMUND NELSON, 74, now frail, a cashmere shawl over his knees. CHURCH BELLS, loud, crash out glorious carillons. A COCKNEY MAID enters, and bobs.

COCKNEY MAID

His Lordship, Your Ladyship.

FANNY rises, excited, expecting Nelson. Enter REAR-ADMIRAL LORD COLLINGWOOD, 40. COLLINGWOOD takes off his hat and puts it down on the side-table.

COLLINGWOOD

Fanny ... *(He kisses her cheek.)*

FANNY

Cuthbert.

COLLINGWOOD

(To Reverend)

How are you sir?

They shake hands. The REVEREND does not get up.

REVEREND

Collingwood, very good to see you. You are well?

COLLINGWOOD

Indeed, and yourself?

REVEREND

Anno Domini, my lord, ano domini. But, thanks to dear Fanny, I endure.

COLLINGWOOD

Isn't it splendid. Bells all over London, celebrating Nelson's achievement. In church, the Bishop was in tears! How is he? Is he recovered? He took a ricochet, did he not? Is he on his feet? May I see him?

FANNY

I'm sorry. *(She is unable to speak.)*

REVEREND

Horatio has been delayed. He is in England – but not in London. There is so much to be done, I am sure.

COLLINGWOOD

No doubt. Will he ... When may we expect him?

ACT TWO

FANNY

(Picks up a letter)

By Thursday. We are to give a dinner for the Prince.
As you know, Horatio was his lieutenant when he was
a midshipman. So – a – a dinner is to be arranged.
Here. You will, of course, be our guest?

COLLINGWOOD

Am I invited? Does he want me?

FANNY

I want you, Cuthbert. Please.

COLLINGWOOD

Then I'll be honoured.

He kisses her hand.

COLLINGWOOD

Heady times, Fanny. We are all swept up. But storms
pass, winds die away. Our task is support.

FANNY

Yes. That is what I intend to do.

COLLINGWOOD

Bravo. *(Bows to the Reverend.)* Your servant, sir.

REVEREND

Good of you to look in, my Lord.

COLLINGWOOD

The honour's mine. I assure you.

FANNY gives him his hat, escorts him to the exit.

He takes her hands.

COLLINGWOOD

Courage and a steady course.

FANNY

I am well trained in it, Cuthbert. I am, after all, married to the navy.

He kisses her cheek and goes. She crosses, tidies the REVEREND'S shawl, takes a book and sits.

The bells peal again, joyously triumphant, and very loud.

Fade to black.

ACT TWO – SCENE ELEVEN

Dining Room – London – Night

Present, at the head of the table, is PRINCE WILLIAM OF HANOVER, with LADY EMMA HAMILTON on his right, and ADMIRAL NELSON, with eye-patch, on his left. FANNY is at the other end with REAR-ADMIRAL COLLINGWOOD on her left and SIR WILLIAM HAMILTON on her right. To his right is CAPTAIN HARDY. To COLLINGWOOD'S left is CAPTAIN TROUBRIDGE. The meal is nearing its end. A FOOTMAN refills glasses with red wine. PRINCE WILLIAM'S glass is huge and he drinks freely.

PRINCE WILLIAM
(To EMMA)

I got them married. Nelson and his little lady there. What a good little soul she is. *(He waves genially to FANNY.)* No fun being a naval wife, don't you know. When I'm Admiral of the Fleet, wives will be allowed passage – well, if their men want them, and we aren't up for a fight. How's that for the troops, Nelson?

NELSON

Need bigger ships, sir.

ACT TWO

PRINCE WILLIAM

Build "em – build "em! I hear one of your ships sank, Sir William – the one full of Greek vases when you had to run for Sicily.

SIR WILLIAM HAMILTON

Alas, yes, Your Highness. A tragedy. Two thousand years of history lost forever.

PRINCE WILLIAM

Never mind. Still got your best treasure, eh? *(Paws EMMA's hand)* You'd trade a fleet for this one – who wouldn't, eh, Nelson?

NELSON

Sir?

PRINCE WILLIAM

Come on man, pass the port – the other hand, other hand – oh, sorry.

NELSON

Not at all, sir. What's an arm between shipmates?

PRINCE WILLIAM

Shipmates – yes! *(He puts an arm round NELSON, engulfing him.)* And none prouder than yours truly. Do you know – *(To EMMA)* this light-footed fox was my lieutenant when I was a midshipman. Best Jimmy I ever served under. Where was it? Atlantic? Pacific?

COLLINGWOOD
(Calls)

Caribbean, sir!

PRINCE WILLIAM

That's right! I took money off you at cards. *(To NELSON)* Pity about the arm. Makes you look lop-sided.

EMMA rises, and sways.

NELSON

Lady Hamilton is not well. Can't you see? She is not well!

FANNY rises – so does SIR WILLIAM HAMILTON. But EMMA waves him back as FANNY takes her arm. FANNY and EMMA go.

NELSON gestures to CAPTAIN HARDY to go and look after EMMA.

HARDY

Excuse me, Sire.

CAPTAIN HARDY exits.

PRINCE WILLIAM

Hardy? Where's he going? What's the matter? Not me, is it? Am I misbehaving?

CAPTAIN TROUBRIDGE

Never sir. Never been known.

PRINCE WILLIAM

Sir William?

SIR WILLIAM HAMILTON

I salute England's finest, sir.

PRINCE WILLIAM

But do you love me? No, no you're a sport. Gentleman – glasses. A toast to the finest looking woman in England. Lady Hamilton!

They toast LADY HAMILTON.

ACT TWO

ALL

Lady Hamilton!

PRINCE WILLIAM

And here's to Nelson, and the battle of the Nile.

They toast NELSON.

ALL

Lord Nelson!

PRINCE WILLIAM

Mind you, I'd have caught that bugger Napoleon at Malta, meself. I know, let's play Cardinal Puff. Come on – what's the matter? Am I misbehaving? (*To NELSON*) No, I adore that woman, so does the Prince of Wales, so watch out. Watch out Sir William. I toast you. There's prestige in being England's premier cuckold.

TROUBRIDGE

Oh Crikey, here we go.

SIR WILLIAM HAMILTON

I prefer the word custodian, sir. I am a collector of beauty but not, I hope, its jailer.

PRINCE WILLIAM

Bloody good. No. Splendid woman. Find one for me will you? Pick me out a filly. Mine's in foal half the time. What are you supposed to do … ?

He falls, drunk, onto the table.

TROUBRIDGE

Never could hold his drink.

SIR WILLIAM HAMILTON

Does the navy bring out the best in him, I wonder?

NELSON

TROUBRIDGE

Keeps him off the streets. Nelson? *(Indicates the port.)*

NELSON rises.

NELSON

I must see to Emma.

He exits.

COLLINGWOOD, SIR WILLIAM and TROUBRIDGE sit in silence.

Fade to black.

ACT TWO – SCENE TWELVE

Fanny's Bedroom – Night

Candlelight. FANNY is in her nightclothes and a lace night cap. NELSON stands apart.

FANNY

So, it's true. *(NELSON is silent.)* I've never seen a woman's body so invaded. She is in milk already!

NELSON turns away.

FANNY

Sir William ...

NELSON

Is not the father.

FANNY

It is too open. You are putting the matter in the public eye. *(He is silent.)* I will speak to Sir William. He must persuade Lady Hamilton to leave London.

ACT TWO

NELSON

No.

FANNY

But your career, your reputation ... You are at risk!

NELSON

I am well acquainted with risk.

FANNY

Risk on behalf of your nation is one thing, Horatio.
Can you not see? We are not high enough in nobility
to be safe from public opinion. One public scandal and
we are done for.

NELSON

When I am with her, I am alive. Undamaged. When
she is there, I am All Right. Can you understand that,
Fanny? How I feel? My feelings?

FANNY

I honour and respect you. I have a great pride in your
achievements, and I suffer for it. I live in anxiety for
your safety, your health, your survival. But feelings
such as you ... No. I have never wanted – sought – felt
the need to – cavort. It is not congenial to me.

ACT TWO – SCENE THIRTEEN

Fanny's Bedroom – Night – Later

Candlelight. FANNY and NELSON pace, crossing each other.

FANNY

I am your Wife! You chose me. Me. Fanny. Am
I nothing? Is virtue, temperance, reason to be

disregarded? I have prayed for your safety from
one dawn to the next, through all the weary days,
months, years of your absence – my very anxieties
have kept me afloat. I have been lonely. Alone.
Without a husband. If we are without issue, well, who
knows? Had we been, as most partners, constantly
together, we were – to be vulgar – never at it. You,
because of your calling, have never been a full
husband to me. You have been husband to your
nation, to your ship, to your comrades in arms, and
I submit to that, but – oh – now for you to come into
town in all your glory, with another woman. And such
a woman! A woman of ...

NELSON

Well?

FANNY

You are not a fool, Horatio. You know of Lady
Hamilton's history. Mistress to Sir Charles Greville,
passed on by him to his uncle, Sir William ...

NELSON

A man who has honoured her with his name.

FANNY

(Trembling)

I ... I admit Lady Hamilton's beauty, her warmth,
kindness – but how can I ... ? Asking me to receive
her at our table. It is Out of Place! Please. Think,
Horace. Can you really intend to throw away
everything you have achieved? I have submitted
to my needs being being down the line, and the
loneliness of my life, which has been made even more
painful by your elevation. Where there was snub now

ACT TWO

there is fawning. I accept all of it with pride in your
achievement. I know that what I offer – the quiet
pursuits of a country life ... yes, I see how little they
must intrude on your glorious, glittering life of fame
and renown. And I wish I thought you the humbler
man for it! Come home, Horace. Please.

Silence.

NELSON

She suits me. We belong in the same world. When I'm
with her I feel at home.

FANNY

(Low)

Please. Think of your family!

NELSON

She is carrying my child.

FANNY's heart breaks. She stoops, lifts a candelabrum, stands and
gazes at him, in shock. NELSON sits, head down, his hand on his
knee. Then he slaps his knee, rises, and goes swiftly.

Fade to black.

ACT TWO – SCENE FOURTEEN

Sitting Room – Nelson and Emma's House – Day

An armchair, sofa, desk, drinks table on which are bottles, glasses
and a bowl of walnuts. Sound of birds twittering.

OLD TOM is telling a story to Nelson's daughter, HORATIA (8), who
is lying on her stomach, head supported on her elbows.

TOM

... so, there we are a-stumbling through the swamp in our smelly old sea boots, with the giant snakes a- snapping and a-snarking and hissing huge gobs of ginger sh–spit and I tells the poor young sailormen to keep their eyes shut lessen they gets spat on and a- done for ...

HORATIA

How could they see where to go if they had their eyes shut?

TOM

They couldn't, could they? So, they open 'em and gets squirted.

HORATIA
(Eagerly)

And killed?

TOM

Worse'n that.

HORATIA

Worse?

TOM

Them that gets spit in the eye by the Giant Snakes of the Mildewy Swamp loses their ...

Enter NELSON. Now 46, his hair is greying. TOM sees him.

TOM

... loses their ... their best Sunday bonnet, and their hair goes out of curl. Morning, sir.

HORATIA runs, jumps up, and NELSON catches her with one arm, and she puts an arm around his neck.

ACT TWO

HORATIA

Papa!

NELSON walks apart with TOM, HORATIA clinging to his neck.

He mutters something to TOM, who listens and nods.

TOM takes HORATIA in his arms, and goes. HORATIA looks back over his shoulder at NELSON, who goes to her for a last kiss. She smiles at him, and then TOM bears her away. EMMA enters, fuller in figure, but as beautiful as ever. They kiss briefly. She ties his stock.

NELSON

Collingwood, calling on us!

EMMA shakes her head.

EMMA

Calling on you because you are needed.

NELSON

So, stay and receive him. Offer congratulations.

EMMA

For a stiff bow and a glance past my shoulder? I shall save us both the embarrassment. In any case *(She laughs)*. Collingwood? Admiral of the Fleet? When we have a Nelson?

NELSON

Oh, Cuthbert's sound enough.

But he breaks away and paces, with his stealthy, light-footed tread.

NELSON

I shall have The Victory.

EMMA

Oh, you will! *(NELSON grins)*

NELSON

With Hardy as Flag Captain.

EMMA

I've packed the medicine chest. Chamomile – Tom will infuse it for you – and laudanum when the headache is bad.

NELSON

The paddock needs re-fencing.

EMMA

I'll see to it.

NELSON

And the river is high already.

EMMA

Re-dig the ditches?

NELSON

Not as exciting as the sea.

NELSON

More companionable, though. Tom's taken Horatia down to bathe.

EMMA

She'll be swimming like an eel by the time you come ashore.

NELSON

I told him to keep her away from the house until the carriage leaves. I don't want her to see me cry.

EMMA

(Kisses him)

Of course not. Not until her wedding day. Then you can cry.

ACT TWO

NELSON

I must finish dressing.

EMMA

And I must disappear.

NELSON

Stay a little longer?

EMMA

No. You're gone from me already.

They embrace. A long, needful embrace.

NELSON

It gets harder. I never thought not to want to be aboard.

EMMA

We are here for you, where we belong – willing as ever to share you with England.

NELSON

My practical woman.

EMMA

And a sailor's doxy. Ready at all hours of the watch.

He laughs, smacks her on the bum, and exits.

EMMA stands, immobile. Then shakes herself awake.

EMMA

(Matter of fact)

Mine eyes smell onions. I shall weep anon.

She goes. The PARLOURMAID shows in ADMIRAL COLLINGWOOD and CAPTAIN HARDY. Then she leaves.

HARDY

So, here we are. Pretty place, sir.

COLLINGWOOD grunts agreement.

> HARDY
> Fine quarters, but the Admiral will be pleased to be aboard. He gets restless ashore.

> COLLINGWOOD
> Yes, yes.

NELSON enters.

> COLLINGWOOD
> Ah!

> NELSON
> Admiral.

> COLLINGWOOD
> Admiral.

> NELSON
> Congratulations on ...

COLLINGWOOD, embarrassed, turns away.

> NELSON
> So – he's on the move?

> HARDY
> At last.

> COLLINGWOOD
> Villeneuve's in Cadiz – and the French Fleet have quit Toulon on Napoleon's orders.

> NELSON
> They're at sea?

> HARDY
> Yes! At last!

ACT TWO

NELSON

Hah! Months of being congratulated by the Admiralty on our blockade when we've been trying to entice the buggers out.

COLLINGWOOD is not amused. NELSON crosses to his desk and picks up dispatches, which he gives to CAPTAIN HARDY.

NELSON

I want decent victualing on the Victory. Six ounces of lemon juice a day with sugar. Leeks, pumpkins, sheep and oranges.

HARDY

Very good.

NELSON

Have a word with stores below – they have the lists.

CAPTAIN HARDY bows and goes.

COLLINGWOOD

Well, Nelson.

NELSON

Well, Admiral.

COLLINGWOOD

Harrumph. Saw your little girl out there.

NELSON

Horatia.

COLLINGWOOD

Fine child.

NELSON

How's Your daughter?

NELSON pours drinks.

COLLINGWOOD

(Comes to life)

Sarah? Oh, she's splendid. What a pity she ... They can't ...

Silence.

NELSON

Congratulations on your elevation.

COLLINGWOOD

Thank you.

NELSON

Remember how I kept you down? I never was a nice man, Cuth. What was it you called me? The little stoat?

COLLINGWOOD

Sea-wolf, I think I said.

NELSON

Remember when I threw dead sailors overboard to fox the French?

COLLINGWOOD shakes his head at the memory.

NELSON

It worked. We fooled them. The mariners left to drift wouldn't have said no.

COLLINGWOOD

To a decent Christian burial?

NELSON

To saving the lives of their shipmates.

COLLINGWOOD

You weren't loved that day.

ACT TWO

NELSON

No, I wasn't. There's the difference between us. You've always settled for the luxury of decency. To me, for a fighting man to crave virtue amounts to treason.

COLLINGWOOD

(Half-rising)

I beg your pardon?

NELSON

You're traitors, Cuth, you and your sort. Oh, you're prepared to risk flesh. You'll haul a man off a rampart, lead a boarding charge, but you won't risk what's in Here *(He strikes his temple)* ... or Here *(He strikes his chest.)* All – gesture.

COLLINGWOOD

That's enough.

NELSON

Cuthbert Collingwood, Admiral of the Fleet. Chosen by committee by the reasonable men in Whitehall.

COLLINGWOOD

I don't respect you, Horace. I never have. I don't approve of your actions. Rash. Dangerous. Murderous.

NELSON

Successful.

COLLINGWOOD

You've been lucky. I don't approve of your tactics, your strategy – nor of your private life.

NELSON

Please – don't ...

COLLINGWOOD

You are a public figure. You shame us. You shame the service. Nonetheless ... Nonetheless, I am prepared to concede that without your freakish forays we might now be wearing the Tricolore and sending signals in French. However, from now on ... *(They eyeball each other.)* From now on ... We'll see.

NELSON refills their glasses.

NELSON

Just so long as you give me my head.

COLLINGWOOD

You'll take it anyway.

They look at each other. And then lift their glasses.

COLLINGWOOD

To a fair wind.

They drink. NELSON pushes a large bowl towards COLLINGWOOD.

NELSON

Walnut?

COLLINGWOOD

(Shakes his head.)

My teeth, alas.

NELSON

Mine too.

They look at each other and laugh ruefully.

Fade Out.

ACT TWO

ACT TWO - SCENE FIFTEEN

Aboard the Victory – Dawn

Sound of surging sea and a high wind. Spotlight on the nameplate of the ship: 'VICTORY.' The HELMSMAN is at the wheel. The BOSUN is swabbing the quarterdeck. TOM is seated on a barrel, making a fender of matted coir. Further fora'rd, JEM and TIMOTHY are looking out to sea. JEM and TIMOTHY cross to TOM.

JEM

Quiet eh, Tom?

TOM

Quiet enough, lads.

Silence between them.

TIMOTHY

It's not dying I'm afeared of.

JEM

Not much!

TIMOTHY

Even losing a leg, or an arm, like himself – it's ... it's ...

TOM

(Indicates his eyes)

It's losing your peepers.

JEM

Aye.

TOM

Don't worry. If'n your face gets blowed in, I'll brain you with a marlinspike.

                    TIMOTHY
                    (Grateful)

Thanks, Tom.

They go silent. Aloft, sails are unreefed and fill with wind.

> *Light change.*

ACT TWO – SCENE SIXTEEN

Nelson's Cabin – Day

NELSON is in his small clothes. TOM, in the background, is laying out his uniform on his bed. NELSON turns.

                    NELSON

Not that one.

                    TOM

Sir?

                    NELSON

Full dress.

TOM looks at him, opens a locker, stows the uniform, and takes out NELSON's full dress uniform. He displays it. NELSON nods.

TOM begins to dress NELSON. Enter CAPTAIN HARDY. He stops short at the sight of NELSON's full splendour laid out on the bed.

                    HARDY

Full dress, sir?

                    NELSON

Why not? The men need to see me.

                    HARDY

You'll need cover.

ACT TWO

NELSON

Cover?

HARDY

There'll be no shortage of volunteers to block the path of sharp-shooters.

NELSON

Who do you think I am?

TOM attends to dressing NELSON.

NELSON

God, I hate war.

HARDY looks at him, surprised.

NELSON

It's wrong. Against nature. Nature is Life, Hardy!

HARDY

And death.

NELSON

Natural rot and accident – that's different. I'm talking of cold destruction. What we are paid to do.

HARDY looks at TOM, mystified. TOM shrugs.

HARDY

What we are paid for is the defence of the realm against savagery and despotism.

NELSON

And how do wars end?

HARDY

One side wins and other side loses.

NELSON

Wars end by men sitting around a table. Look at me. The hero. A disabled, disfigured man, and for what? For men to sit around a table.

HARDY

(Trying to be jolly. To TOM)

Is he often like this?

TOM

Couldn't say, sir.

NELSON

I chose the wrong profession. There are only three professions, Hardy. Teaching. Medicine – and Politics.

HARDY

Politics?

NELSON

I never had any doubts. To be a fighting man – to risk body – and soul. But, on reflection ... Why? Why risk this. *(He strikes himself on the chest.)* The only repository of thought, when thought – thought alone – can solve the conflict.

HARDY

Tame wild animals with reason?

NELSON

By vote. By law. By prevention. To give despotism its head is political vandalism. Wars can, should, must be won at the table. And Never Happen.

HARDY

I wish I shared your faith in the skill, not to mention the probity of politicians.

ACT TWO

NELSON

It's not a matter of virtue. It's a matter of corruption. Of how – when to corrupt. Or consent to be corrupted.

HARDY

The end justifies the means.

NELSON

That's just it. What ends? What means? There's the responsibility. In the politics – all in the politics. I've been a fool. A brute lackey waist-deep in entrails and for what? Where's the national profit in blowing a man to pieces, piercing the heart, his back-bone ... Useless, mindless, unbearable waste. The reason to elide killing is because it is irrelevant. Unprofitable. Not in our interest. I am a family man now. I tell you, Hardy, after this battle, it's Parliament for me. Time to belay bomb, cutlass and cannon for a more potent weapon. Words. Words, Hardy! Why has it taken me so long? The action's not offshore. It's in Whitehall. I can hardly wait to be suspected for acting – for not acting – despised for changing sides, disliked for refusing to sign, loathed for signing, for playing both against the middle, dissembling – rewarding the weak, neglecting the strong, favouring the cheat and ignoring the honest man. And all, all in the name of the people – for their children, their dependents and their descendants. Breathtaking. I can't wait for the game to begin. I shall be good at it.

He holds out his arm for his coat. HARDY puts it on.

Four bells ring. HARDY stands back as TOM hands NELSON his hat.

NELSON exits, followed by HARDY. TOM stands, thoughtful. Then he straightens the bed swiftly, and goes.

Blackout.

ACT TWO – SCENE SEVENTEEN

The Deck of the Victory – Day

Sound of waves and wind. Bosun's whistle.

The COXSWAIN and SAILOR hoist a sail. The HELMSMAN is at the wheel. CAPTAIN TROUBRIDGE is on the poop deck.

TROUBRIDGE
(Shouts)
Captain to quarterdecks, gunners to gun-decks,
surgeons stand by, marines to upper decks,
lieutenants to gun-decks!

ADMIRAL NELSON, CAPTAIN HARDY and TOM appear on the quarterdeck in close conference. They are joined by CAPTAIN TROUBRIDGE. Enter the BOSUN.

BOSUN
(To NELSON)
Sorry, sir. About the signal. Could I use "expects" instead of "confides" – only "expects" is just the one flag, sir. Makes a clearer message.

NELSON thinks.

NELSON
Expects. Very good.

BOSUN
Thank you, sir.

ACT TWO

He salutes and goes. NELSON returns to his staff. CAPTAIN HARDY unfurls a chart. They confer, heads together. The BOSUN enters and flies the flag signal. All look up.

NELSON

Collingwood will say what the devil's all that for?

The OTHERS laugh, then move off quietly, leaving NELSON alone.

He looks at the chart, puts it aside and scans the horizon.

He paces. A stillness falls. NELSON paces.

Then he is motionless, slight and frail and colourful in his full uniform. His back to us, he gazes out to sea. Now there is an uncanny silence. The scene is frozen and becomes a painting in glorious light.

THE END.

NELSON

Cast breakdown

1. HORATIO NELSON
2. CUTHBERT COLLINGWOOD
3. LADY EMMA HAMILTON – LADY HOTHAM
4. PRINCE WILLIAM OF HANOVER – SPANISH ADMIRAL
5. LORD HOOD – SIR JOHN HERBERT – KING FERDINAND – CAPTAIN TROUBRIDGE
6. FANNY NELSON – QUEEN MARIE CAROLINA
7. REVEREND NELSON – SIR WILLIAM HAMILTON
8. HARDY – CAPTAIN KINGSMILL – SPANISH CAPTAIN
9. TOM
10. HORATIA
11. BOSUN – EQUERRY – BATH RESIDENT #1 – CHAMBERLAIN – SPANIARD #1 – BUTLER – MARINE CAPTAIN
12. COXSWAIN – SAM – SNOB #2 – SPANISH SHARPSHOOTER – SPANIARD #2 – FOOTMAN – TIMOTHY
13. SAILOR – DANIEL – BATH RESIDENT #2 – COURTIER #2 – GUEST #1 – JEM

ASMs

1. HELMSMAN – SNOB #1 – COURTIER #1 – WEDDING GUEST – SPANISH ASSASSIN – SPANIARD #2 – GUEST #2
2. MAID – ITALIAN MAID – COCKNEY MAID – PARLOURMAID

NOT JOAN THE MUSICAL

A love story in two acts

NOT JOAN THE MUSICAL

CHARACTERS

FLORIA
JUNE

NOT JOAN THE MUSICAL

ACT ONE

ACT ONE SCENE ONE

The living-room of a semi-detached Edwardian house in Wimbledon. Old and comfortable furniture, a rose-covered sofa, pictures and books, music centre and television.

JUNE is sitting, legs up, reading. She is in her 30's/40's, wears a plain skirt and sweater and flat shoes. With a messy haircut, she ought to look like nothing, but there's an angularity about her, an edge. She has a style of her own. She reads for some time, then rises and exits. She returns – with a cup of tea – and continues to read. A sudden SQUEAL OF BRAKES, and the sound of a CRASH. Startled, JUNE leaps to her feet, throws down her book, and runs out. A door bangs offstage. The sound of voices.

JUNE enters supporting a FIGURE in leathers and helmet. She sits the person down gently, then leaps across for her mobile phone.

> FIGURE

What are you doing?

> JUNE

I'm calling an ambulance.

> FIGURE

Don't!

JUNE is arrested by the figure doffing gloves, boots, helmet and leathers. Out of which steps a dark, vivid WOMAN in a maroon jumpsuit with a white faux-fur collar. This is FLORIA. JUNE helps

her to sit, bends on one knee, and feels the ankle. FLORIA relaxes.
She looks around, taking in the room.

>   FLORIA
>
> This your place?
>
>   JUNE
>
> There doesn't appear to be anything broken. Yes.

FLORIA rises, and tries her leg.

>   FLORIA
>   (in pain.)
>
> Bastard!
>
>   JUNE
>
> I'm sorry.

FLORIA hobble around.

>   FLORIA
>
> Bloody Volvo cut me up. Forced me on the pavement.
> Fucking black bags everywhere!
>
>   JUNE
>
> Oh dear. That was me. They're for the recycling.
> Waste paper.
>
>   FLORIA
>
> How many people have you got living here!
>
>   JUNE
>
> Just me.
>
>   FLORIA
>
> On your own?
>
>   JUNE
>
> Since my parents died.

FLORIA sticks out her hand.

ACT ONE

FLORIA

Floria de Winter.

JUNE

June Rosen.

FLORIA

You know, you look quite different when you smile.

JUNE stares at her, confused.

Blackout.

MUSIC.

ACT ONE SCENE TWO

JUNE and FLORIA enter from the kitchen. FLORIA has a bowl and spoon, sits and eats.

FLORIA

This soup is heavenly.

JUNE

It's from the Ritz.

FLORIA looks up. JUNE laughs.

JUNE

Ray, my next-door-neighbour, is a sous-chef.

FLORIA

Handy guy.

JUNE

No, Ray's a woman. (*Doubtful.*) Well ...

FLORIA, still eating, looks around the room.

FLORIA

So, June ... What do you do when you're not eating left-overs from the Ritz?

JUNE

Me?

FLORIA

No, Maria Callas.

JUNE

I'm a tax consultant.

FLORIA looks up, dropping her bowl. JUNE offers her a tissue to wipe her face. FLORIA lifts her face for JUNE to wipe it.

So, JUNE does it. FLORIA rises. She prowls, picking up things, and books, for close inspection.

FLORIA

Accountant, huh?

JUNE

Not very exciting, I'm afraid.

FLORIA

Oh, I don't know. Every woman needs an accountant in her life. Is this a Sickert?

JUNE rises and joins FLORIA. They gaze at a sizeable painting.

JUNE

My grandparents bought it in Holland on their way here in '39.

FLORIA
(Sits)

Jewish?

JUNE nods.

ACT ONE

FLORIA

They got out, your family?

JUNE

Some of them.

FLORIA stares at the Sickert painting.

FLORIA

"Yearn. And yearn.

And remember –

Laughter is allowable.

Advisable.

To be preferred to the alternative."

JUNE turns.

JUNE

You're a poet.

FLORIA

Of course.

JUNE

I knew it. I sensed it. Would I – would I know your work?

FLORIA

I publish rarely. Poetry is from a deep well.

JUNE

Oh indeed. Too deep sometimes – look at Ezra Pound!

FLORIA

Who?

JUNE is puzzled, then feels that FLORIA is making a sophisticated joke and laughs.

JUNE

An actual live poet!

FLORIA

And playwright.

JUNE

Playwright? Heavens. Are you ... Are you working on anything at the moment?

FLORIA

Is the Pope Catholic? I'm doing a piece about Joan.

JUNE

Of Arc?

FLORIA

No, Bethnal Green.

JUNE

Sorry.

FLORIA

Been done before, of course, by GBS, but what does a blabbermouth Irish journalist know about Joan of Arc? Apart from the fact that they were both virgins.

JUNE laughs.

FLORIA

Totally unauthentic.

JUNE

You see Joan from the woman's point of view?

FLORIA

You could say that. Whichever way you cut it, she was show-biz.

ACT ONE

JUNE

What is your play called?

FLORIA

Joan the Musical.

JUNE

(Offering FLORIA a biscuit)

Tell me, do you – I mean – her voices – Joan – do you actually think she ... Will your approach be ... ?

FLORIA is head down in the biscuit tin.

JUNE

... there are those who say she was no more than a puppet, used by powerful ... And, of course, some say she escaped the fire.

FLORIA

(Looks up)

Not in my musical she doesn't. Well, it depends on the budget. I may have to send her to the Crusades ...

SHOUTING offstage. It makes FLORIA jump up.

JUNE

Sorry. It's Ray, my neighbour.

More SHOUTING. They wait for it to stop.

JUNE

It's probably the postman.

FLORIA

Why, what's he done?

JUNE

Nothing. He's a chap. Ray doesn't like men. One tried to kiss her once.

> FLORIA

Is she often noisy like that?

> JUNE

Sometimes.

> FLORIA

Only I need somewhere quiet to work. Have you got a room going?

JUNE looks at her, bewildered.

> FLORIA

You know, you should wear a hat. You've got the face for it.

> *Light change.*

MUSIC.

ACT ONE SCENE THREE

JUNE is at the table, doing accounts. She writes a letter and stamps it. She eats a sandwich.

> FLORIA
>
> *(From the sofa)*
>
> We're out of coffee.

JUNE nods, adds it to her list.

> FLORIA

Oh, and get a coffee grinder and some beans.

> JUNE

Don't you like instant?

ACT ONE

                    FLORIA

Instant coffee? (*Sits up.*) Actually, the best way is to
buy green beans and roast them. On a tin plate.
Over an open fire. Like the Sudanese.

                    JUNE

But won't that be an awful bore?

                    FLORIA

You'll soon get used to it.

MUSIC.

ACT ONE SCENE FOUR

JUNE and FLORIA enter.

FLORIA opens shopping bags, and tries on new boots. She throws
a bag over to JUNE. JUNE opens the bag, finds trainers. FLORIA
gestures to her to try them on – so she does.

                    FLORIA

Well?

                    JUNE

I feel a fool. (*She teeters timidly.*)

                    FLORIA

Wear them!

She throws a new scarf around her neck. She turns, and begins to
teach JUNE the slow foxtrot.

MUSIC

ACT ONE SCENE FIVE

FLORIA walks about, looking for anything of value, and pausing to inspect the Sickert, while talking on her mobile.

> FLORIA
>
> ... and we guarantee no home visits. Take your time filling out the forms. Remember, it's in your interest to select the model most suitable for your hubbie. It's all explained on page forty-one ... No, the pink form – which also sets out the favourable terms for this month only. You won't find anything to touch us on the High Street. But, as I say, we don't spend money on bricks and mortar, we spend it on our customers. We care about you. We're on your side!

She listens, 'phone under her ear, and makes rapid notes.

> FLORIA
>
> ... yes, the remedial with the tilting system and the automatic riser ... fifteen hundred, all inclusive, postage and delivery free. All you need to do is sign at the bottom of pages 3, 5, 52, 54 and 55 ... and 55, yes ... Good. Now I want you to promise me, Mrs – ah – (*She checks her notes.*) Proctor – that you'll get this off to us today. Your husband's back is as important to us as it is to you, and you don't want to miss out on our special offer and the free gift of ... (*Checks her notes*) ... the set of barbecue skewers for the patio. Have you got a pen handy? That's all right. I'll hang on. (*She waits, humming.*) Are you there? Good! One of the best decisions of your life. Have you got a stamp? Fine. Thank you. We aim to please ... And to you ... All the best.

ACT ONE

She puts down the mobile phone quickly as JUNE enters.

> JUNE
>
> Who was that?
>
> FLORIA
>
> My ex. A bitch.

ACT ONE SCENE SIX

JUNE is on the telephone.

> JUNE
>
> I agree with you, Elaine. There is no point. Not for you, not for me, not for anyone. We're all in the same boat. You've had a knock – a bad knock. The way you feel is normal and right. An honest reaction to tragedy. You will get over it. In the end. Because you must and because, in the end, time will do it for you. Because time moves on, and takes you with it whether you want it or not. People try to stay with their grief as a sort of loyalty to the lost one. Sometimes I feel we're holding the loved ones back when we do that. I lost my parents in an accident ... Yes, I did ... Yes. It can help to share ... Well, none of us knows that ... I can't help you there. It's not what the Samaritans are for. We're not here to tell you what to do. Well, sometimes, offer alternatives I suppose ... Yes, make our own decisions. ... Yes, yes, oh yes, I agree ... Absolutely not. It's your right to grieve. And be angry. And blame other people. And yourself. And God. Of course you can't think of another baby at this time! ... Oh, Elaine, life is so

precious ... I agree ... Oh, I do. I know ... I feel that
too. I suppose we all do. That's it. We're meant to care.
If we didn't, we'd be ... Absolutely ... Of course! ...
Exactly. Keep busy. There's nothing like it ... Why
not? Start with something simple. (*Listens, nodding.*)
They say slow-cooking is better for you. I might try
that myself ... Thanks, Elaine. All the best. You've
got a big heart ... I agree. Women are stronger than
men ... Okay. And to you. Goodbye for now ... You
know where we are. 'Bye.

She lies back, exhausted. FLORIA enters, pulls JUNE to her feet, then throws JUNE's jacket at her.

They leave.

MUSIC.

ACT ONE SCENE SEVEN

FLORIA and JUNE enter. JUNE has had her hair cut.

FLORIA takes a hat from a bag. JUNE unwillingly puts it on. FLORA tweaks it to the right angle. JUNE gazes at herself in the glass.

FLORIA

It's you. It's you!

JUNE gazes at herself.

JUNE

All right. But you won't make me have one of those make-overs, will you?

FLORIA

Of course not.

ACT ONE

JUNE

They always look better before.

FLORIA

Come here.

She swings JUNE around in a slow foxtrot.

MUSIC.

ACT ONE SCENE EIGHT

JUNE and FLORA are watching Gérard Depardieu's last speech in 'Cyrano' on TV. JUNE switches off, and blows her nose. FLORIA finishes sobbing.

JUNE

I love French films. You're allowed to be sexy, even
When you're old and ugly.

FLORIA

Speak for yourself.

Pause.

JUNE

Floria?

FLORIA

Yuh?

JUNE

Are you happy here?

FLORIA

Why?

JUNE

I just wondered.

FLORIA

Sure.

JUNE hands her a box.

FLORIA

What's this?

FLORIA dives in, and takes out a necklace of heavy stones.

JUNE

Aquamarines.

FLORIA

(Weighing them.)

How much did they cost?

JUNE

Mind your own business. They're a celebration.
You've been here six months.

FLORIA

(Puts on the necklace.)

Mmm.

JUNE

They're sandblasted.

FLORIA

Not bad.

FLORIA lies back. JUNE looks at her fondly.

MUSIC.

ACT ONE

ACT ONE SCENE NINE

FLORIA at the table.

JUNE enters, wearing an office suit, carrying her briefcase.

JUNE

Oh, sorry. (*She makes to tip-toe off.*) You're working.

FLORIA

Where'd you get that idea?

JUNE

Well ... sorry.

FLORIA

Say that word again, I'll slit your throat.

JUNE

Oh, yes. I do see. It must be maddening.

FLORIA

Every time you want to get off on saying sorry, say 'shit.'

JUNE

I'll make a note of that.

She turns to go. FLORA looks up.

FLORIA

I'm blocked.

JUNE

Sorry? I mean – shit?

FLORIA

I've got writer's block.

JUNE

Oh. Is there anything I can do?

FLORIA

I doubt it. Anyway, what's the point? To get Joan to Edinburgh for the Festival will take at least ten thou.

JUNE

Ten thousand? Pounds?

FLORIA

And that's without paying the actors.

JUNE

Oh dear. Is Edinburgh vital? As a showcase for Joan?

FLORIA

Absolutely. Window on the world for exciting new work.

JUNE

I see.

FLORIA

Of course, it's a risk. All art is a risk. Life is a risk.

JUNE

I understand that.

FLORIA

Do you?

FLORIA crumples. JUNE surveys her – makes up her mind – crosses to her desk, takes out her cheque-book, writes a check, and hands it to her.

FLORIA

What? What's this?

She takes the cheque and reads it.

ACT ONE

FLORIA

Oh.

JUNE

Twelve thousand. There are always extras.

FLORIA

Twelve thousand pounds? Is this a loan?

JUNE

No. A gift.

FLORIA

A gift? Who from?

JUNE

From me. To you.

FLORIA

Is this for real?

JUNE

I don't think it will bounce.

FLORIA

We-ell. Fantastic. Thanks.

MUSIC.

ACT ONE SCENE TEN

FLORIA is on her mobile.

FLORIA

Cynthia? I'll have the coat. For cash. Yes. Bye.
(She dials again, uses posh voice.) Mr Beaufort?
It's Jessica Fitzwilliam ... Sorry to have kept you

waiting. I'll be in today to settle up ... Yes, well, I've
been burying my mother ... Yes, goodbye. (*She dials
again.*) Sonya, it's me. I need five musicians ... How
should I know? Medieval! And a bass guitar for
the fire scene ... See you. (*Dials again.*) Inez – get a
microwave and some sleeping bags ... What? (*She
listens.*) What?! Fucking hell, Inez, you are a genius!
(*Gives a yelp of triumph.*) How many? ... Too small.
Not enough room for producers, agents and journos –
let alone punters. This is a musical for fuck's sake ...
So, open the balcony after the inspectors have
been ... Good. Great. What?! ... Oh well, if we have
to. (*She listens.*) Finished. I just have to sort out the
Nuns' Chorus, and figure out their names ... Sister
Conception, Sister Emaciata etc. Nobody wants Nun 1
or Nun 2 on their CV ... Okay, bell me.

MUSIC.

ACT ONE SCENE ELEVEN

JUNE enters in jeans and trainers. She puts on Radio 3. It is the chorus from the last act of FIGARO. She sings along as she takes off her jacket. She looks at herself in the mirror.

A HORRENDOUS BANGING on the wall. She turns off the music.

FLORIA enters. She's wearing a pale, camel coat, belted a la Dietrich, a black fedora, flash boots, and carries a silver-headed cane.

FLORIA

Tara!

ACT ONE

JUNE

Floria! You look stunning!

FLORIA

You like?

She displays her new clothes.

JUNE

You look ... expensive!

FLORIA takes out a small bottle of champagne, and pours it.

FLORIA

Celebration time. Inez has found us a space!

JUNE

She hasn't! Where? In Edinburgh?

FLORIA

No, Cleveland, Ohio. It's right next to the Fringe Club! We'll do late shows. Catch the drunks as they come out. Whee!

She swings JUNE off her feet.

JUNE

I can't believe it.

FLORIA

It's a disused synagogue – two hundred seater. Inez is setting up a package deal.

JUNE

Package deal?

FLORIA

We share with some Chilean nose flutes and a group called The Tapping Gays.

NOT JOAN THE MUSICAL

              JUNE

Share?

              FLORIA

Not at the same time, dumbo.

              JUNE

Oh, sorry. I mean – shit.

              FLORIA

They play matinées. Celebration dinner?

              JUNE

Lovely! I'll get my coat.

              FLORIA

Nah. You cook. Let's have curried chicken and trifle. With glacé cherries.

              JUNE

You are an infant.

              FLORA

I'll go out and get some wine.

She holds out her hand. JUNE gives her money and she goes.

JUNE, tired, exits to cook.

MUSIC.

ACT ONE SCENE TWELVE

FLORIA and JUNE after dinner. Silence. JUNE crosses, and refills FLORIA's glass. FLORIA does not drink.

              JUNE

Is it the second act? Can I help?

ACT ONE

FLORIA

You can help by shutting up.

JUNE

I'm sorr...

FLORIA

How am I supposed to work? How the hell am I s'posed to get into the dreamy imaginative state I need to write, when my head is like a boiled pig's head from worrying about money!

JUNE

But I thought we'd solved...

FLORIA

I'm a writer, not a producer. I need a producer. Where's my producer? I need nourishment – not some cunt who sits on her arse telling me the opening of my play is crap.

JUNE

I didn't say that!

FLORIA

You said the opening of the play was crap.

JUNE

No, Floria. I didn't say that. You said it. You said the opening of the play was crap. You said it wasn't ineffable.

FLORIA
(Moody)
What was I on? The trouble with this house is there's a philistine atmosphere.

She knocks back her brandy, and staggers offstage. JUNE stands, miserable. Then decides on action, goes to her desk, finds a yellow lawyer's pad and a pen.

She sits down on the sofa, with the pad on her knees, and starts to write.

MUSIC.

ACT ONE SCENE THIRTEEN

FLORIA, in a long T-shirt, appears.

> FLORIA
>
> What are you doing?
>
> JUNE
>
> Writing.
>
> FLORIA
>
> It's three o'clock in the morning.
>
> JUNE
>
> I'm trying to help. With Joan. The opening. Trying to make it ineffable.
>
> FLORIA
>
> What!?

FLORIA seems affronted. She walks about, irritable. JUNE puts the pad down, apologetically, and looks up at her.

> FLORIA
>
> Okay. So, what have you got?

JUNE clears her throat nervously.

ACT ONE

JUNE

(Mutters)

"I don't want to be married ... "

FLORIA

What? I can't hear you. Get up.

JUNE

Floria, I am not an actress ...

FLORIA

Get up!

JUNE gets up, and stands miserably.

JUNE

(Low)

"I don't want to be married."

FLORA

(Sing-song)

Can't hear you!

JUNE

"I don't want to be married. (*She looks upwards.*) I can't be a wife. I'm not bleeding yet. Tell me what to do! Yesterday, water danced on the ceiling. Plates flew like birds. The walls quivered and sang! Please! They'll tie me down for a madwoman."

She kneels, hands clasped, gazing upwards.

JUNE

Oh Mary, Mother of God. Is it because I'm disobedient?

Silence. JUNE waits.

FLORIA

Look. Look, I know you're trying to help.

JUNE

Sorry. I mean ...

FLORIA

This is a musical for fuck's sake. (*She sings:*)
"Joan, Joan
Crossing the Rhone
Alone
Without a phone
Frozen to the bone
Without a moan."
(*Glances at JUNE.*) What's the matter?

JUNE

Nothing.

FLORIA

This isn't a piece of fascism for phonus balonus uber-pseuds. Fucking middle-class directors on the subsidized tit, laying trips on proles with matey smiles as they spend the punters' taxes on getting themselves laid. When were they ever out on the street? What do they know? June, this is a musical, for Christ's sake! Out there! Up against Brad – Keanu – Elton – Sting! When did you get off the train, for fuck's sake!

JUNE

I didn't know what you wanted. If you could just tell me what you want ...

FLORIA

I'll tell you what I want. I want to be rich and famous. I want to be so famous I pay a publicity agent to keep my name out of the papers. I want a table at the Ivy. I want to sponsor charity events with Ned Sherrin.

ACT ONE

I want to advise Cherie Blair on hair, go snorkeling with Celine. Diss with Julia Roberts! (*She grabs JUNE's script and waves it at her.*) And I want to be so loaded that I need a firm twice your size and three times more dodgy to do my taxes!

JUNE

You said you wanted feeling ...

FLORIA

Feeling? Sure! People getting their rocks off! What do you think sells decking units? Bums! Tits! June. Theatre is dead. Defunct. Gone to its Maker. Up the Swannee. Down the drain. Over the hill. Six feet under. Don't – please – for the love of Larry, give me live theatre!

JUNE

Then why are you writing for the stage?

FLORIA

It's an outlet! The Edinburgh Festival is a showcase! It opens doors! Bloody Scotland, for three weeks a year, gets off its haggis bum. Think of all the people who've made it from Edinburgh! Rowan Atkinson. Stephen Fry. Madonna ...

JUNE

Are you sure?

FLORIA

We'll do three weeks in Edinburgh – then a tour.

JUNE

Tour?

FLORIA

Inez is fixing dates.

JUNE

Inez will run a tour ... of Joan?

FLORIA

Are you kidding? Inez? A woman who drove her car into the sea last week? We're trying for Kash Allen – if we can get her. She doesn't come cheap.

JUNE

And the money will stretch to ... ?

FLORIA

No way. We need more funding. Pronto.

JUNE

My twelve thousand?

FLORIA

A drop in the ocean.

Silence.

FLORIA

I could try Jeremy.

JUNE

Who's Jeremy?

FLORIA

A trustafarian. Notting Hill masochist.

FLORIA gets up. Dials.

FLORIA

Jeremy? ... What?

She waits. Then clicks off.

FLORIA

Misdial. I got Buckingham Palace.

ACT ONE

JUNE

What did they say?

FLORIA

They put me on hold.

FLORIA paces. Shakes her head.

FLORIA

Nah. Last time he slashed his wrists. I don't want to kill the guy. Life before art.

JUNE

Oh Floria, you're wonderful! I've never met anyone like you. You inhabit a different world. It's like a parallel universe.

FLORIA scowls at her.

JUNE

There must be something we can do!

FLORIA

You could sell this place.

JUNE

I'm sorry?

FLORIA

The house. Sell the house.

JUNE

My house? Sell my house?

FLORIA

I know it's where your people came when they got out of Nazi-land, but that was then. This is now.

JUNE

Floria!

FLORIA

You don't need a place this size. It's too far out, there's nowhere to park, there isn't a deli in sight, and Ray makes your life a misery. How am I supposed to work with Godzilla hammering on the walls every night?

JUNE

I know. But I couldn't, Floria. It's my home.

FLORIA

It's not where you are, it's who you are. Where you sleep isn't the point. Art is the point. Take a chance.

JUNE

I can't, Floria. I can't sell my house.

FLORIA

Get a mortgage then.

JUNE shakes her head.

JUNE

No.

FLORIA

Why not?

JUNE

I know how mortgages work.

FLORIA

There must be something you can sell.

Silence. JUNE rises, crosses to the Sickert and gazes at it.

FLORIA watches her, then rises and stands at JUNE's shoulder.

JUNE

I've always loved those strange, inky browns. They look like weather.

ACT ONE

FLORIA waits.

JUNE

English weather.

FLORIA waits.

JUNE takes down the painting.

MUSIC.

ACT ONE SCENE FOURTEEN

JUNE and FLORIA are standing at the table, collating copies of the play.

JUNE

I dreamt of Tom Cruise last night.

FLORIA

Was he wearing Armani? If he was, you're due for a tax rebate.

JUNE

Really?

FLORIA has made a mess of her scripts. JUNE sorts them out.

FLORIA

I'm worried about the Nun's Chorus.

JUNE sorts. FLORIA prowls.

FLORIA

If only they could sing! Then there's the fire. Inez knows a great pyrotechnics guy, but he's not out till next month.

FLORIA marches out

JUNE

Where are you going . . . ?

FLORIA comes back in her camel coat, and the hat.

JUNE

What are you doing?

FLORIA

I need to get past the doorman.

JUNE

Where are you going?

FLORIA

To burgle Jeremy's flat.

JUNE

Floria!

FLORIA goes. JUNE, happy, stacks the scripts. She crosses, puts on a dance CD, and dances. RAY bangs on the wall.

JUNE turns off the CD but lifts her arms in happiness, and goes.

MUSIC.

ACT ONE SCENE FIFTEEN

JUNE and FLORIA in workman's boiler suits.

They manhandle on theatre baskets, pikes, helmets, a horse's head, a long trumpet, some armour, and bunches of faggots.

They sit on the baskets. JUNE consults her lists.

FLORIA

When is the lorry due?

ACT ONE

JUNE

Eleven. Good luck, darling.

FLORIA

No. You should say: 'Break a leg.'

JUNE

Oh yes, sorry. Break a leg.

FLORIA

I need a taller Dauphin. He's too short.

JUNE

It makes him look vulnerable.

FLORIA

It makes me look vulnerable.

They kiss tenderly. FLORIA goes off. JUNE steps out of her boiler suit. She is in a shirt, and trousers. She takes her lists and checks the props, humming to herself. FLORIA enters, now wearing a long skirt with a decorative top and Navaho necklaces in profusion, serious earrings, amazing boots, and a jewelled bandeau low over her brow. JUNE is open-mouthed.

FLORIA

What do you think?

JUNE

Stunning. Absolutely stunning.

FLORIA

I'll be on show ...

JUNE

Absolutely!

FLORIA

The public expect some sort of look. I can't bear artists who disappoint the imagination. Those too-posh--to-push phonies.

JUNE

You look wonderful.

FLORIA

Yup. Could you get my bags down?

JUNE exits. FLORIA looks at costumes from the costume basket- and experiments with a flowing stole. JUNE staggers in with two huge suitcases. Then she goes and returns with more baggage.

JUNE

You did mean all of this?

FLORIA

Any objection?

JUNE

(Breathless with exertion.)

No.

FLORIA

I can't wear the same gear twice.

JUNE

Of course not.

FLORIA

And there's the doubling up.

JUNE

Sorry?

ACT ONE

FLORIA

I have this mobile face. I'm what the French call journalière. I look different every day. So, I need alternatives.

JUNE

I see.

FLORIA

You're lucky. You look the same all the time.

FLORIA puts the stole back in the basket.

FLORIA

And there'll be interviews. TV, radio – business meetings. I've got to look right.

JUNE

Ralph Lauren?

FLORIA

No way. Too beachy. Nicole Fahri.

JUNE

And Betty Jackson for the first night?

FLORIA

Or the charity preview. I can't make up my mind for the premiere. The DK or the Chalayan? But I might keep that for the wrap party. You'll have to help me. Be cruel. Don't let me make a tit of myself.

JUNE

Okay. Will Sonya do your hair?

FLORIA

Ugh, no! She has no left hand. (*Slight pause.*) Marchise.

JUNE

Marchise? Is her English any better?

FLORIA

Only when she's drunk. (*She looks at her watch again.*) Well ...

JUNE

Well? Are you nervous?

FLORIA

I'm shitting myself.

JUNE

Me too.

FLORIA

At least it's not boring.

JUNE

Oh, it's not boring!

FLORIA

Where are they? Where's the lorry? They should be here by now!

JUNE looks at her watch.

JUNE

Another five minutes.

JUNE crosses. She pours two brandies.

JUNE

To you.

FLORIA
(*Holding up glass*)

To me.

ACT ONE

JUNE

Success.

FLORIA

Success.

The DOORBELL rings very loud. It makes them jump.

FLORIA thrusts her glass at JUNE, grabs up the stole and throws it over her shoulders.

FLORIA
(Displaying.)

Okay?

JUNE

Superb.

JUNE picks up the smaller bags.

FLORIA

What are you going to wear?

She exits with a flourish before JUNE can answer. JUNE laughs.

JUNE
(Calls)

Break a leg!

She looks round at the props, then exits with the costume basket.

She returns – and staggers off with the large suitcases.

MUSIC.

Fade to black.

END OF ACT ONE

ACT TWO

ACT TWO SCENE ONE

The Sitting Room.

A burst of heavy-metal from RAY, offstage. JUNE enters, and bangs on the wall. The volume goes up. JUNE leaves.

The MUSIC stops.

FLORIA enters wearing a horrible old dressing gown. Her hair is a mess. She throws herself on the sofa, and gropes for her cigarettes.

JUNE enters, and gives her a cigarette and a light.

The TELEPHONE rings. JUNE answers it.

JUNE

Hello? Oh, Sonya .... Yes, we came back yesterday ... I know, we were booked for eighteen performances ... No audiences, I'm afraid. There was so much competition ... Uh, two at the first performance. One at the second. Just me for the third.

FLORIA gets up and leaves.

JUNE

Sonya, I'm at my wits' end. Floria's in a dreadful state. She's in torment!

RAY's MUSIC starts up again. JUNE crosses, and bangs on the wall.

JUNE
(Yells)
Ray, will you shut the fuck up! Shut up!

The MUSIC stops.

ACT TWO

JUNE

Sorry, Sonya. Has she what? ... Tried slashing her
wrists yet? What do you mean? ... I don't know what
you mean ... Slashing her wrists?

FLORIA enters, and grabs the phone from JUNE.

FLORIA

Fuck off, bitch! Keep your long nose out of it! ...
What? You wouldn't know a relationship if it smashed
you in the face .... What do you mean, what have
I given her? I happen to be extremely emotionally
generous to the point of penury! ... Au contraire. It's
my fucking heart that's ...

A surge of MUSIC from RAY. JUNE bangs. It stops.

FLORIA

Oh, fuck off back to Shepherd's Bush! I hope your dog
dies! ... What? ... Good!

She slams the phone down and throws herself on the sofa. JUNE
crosses to the table, where she sits down and goes through the
post – throwing junk mail and mail-order catalogues into the bin.

FLORIA

It was the wrong gig! (*Pause.*) All those awful comedy
acts. (*Pause.*) What I wrote was poetry!
(*Pause.*) I write a piece of lyrical poetry and what do
I get for my debut? A bat-shit morgue next to a
karaoke pub with shit-faced scrotum Scotsmen
vomiting over their shoes.

Silence.

JUNE

Would you care for anything? Food? Drink?

No response.

JUNE
I could get a takeaway.

There is no response, so JUNE continues struggling with the bills.

Silence.

JUNE
We've got another pop-star on the books. His wife breeds miniature schnauzers. Not a good idea. It has to be from the runt of the litter. Look at Dennis – Sonya's dog.

FLORIA
It's dead.

JUNE
Dead? Dead? When?

FLORIA
Just now.

JUNE
Heavens – what happened?

FLORIA
It died.

Silence.

FLORIA
Flop. Flop. Flop. Flop.

JUNE
Darling, everyone has failures. Look at Noel Coward. Look at poor Tennessee Williams ...

FLORIA
Flop.

ACT TWO

JUNE

Don't.

FLORIA

Flop. Flop. Flop. Flop. Flop!

Silence. FLORIA, hearing a sound, turns. JUNE is crying.

JUNE

Sorry.

She blows her nose.

JUNE

Oh, Floria.

FLORIA

At least you'll be able to say that you were, for a brief moment, a minute cog in the life of an artist. You brushed, infinitesimally, against the universe of the imagination.

JUNE

And I'm grateful for that. I am. If you knew how much! I didn't exist before I knew you.

FLORIA

Don't get too invested.

JUNE

I'm afraid it's rather too late for that now.

Silence.

JUNE

You're not thinking of leaving? (*Pause.*) Floria?

FLORIA

Hemingway said it. "Don't do anything for too damn long."

Silence.

> **JUNE**
>
> I'll sell the house. (*Pause.*) If I sold the house, we could set up a new production of Joan. Arrange a tour.

> **FLORIA**
>
> Don't bother.

> **JUNE**
>
> Why not?

> **FLORIA**
>
> It's crap.

JUNE is shocked. FLORIA starts to laugh. JUNE joins in.

They laugh.

> **JUNE**
>
> Oh, Floria, you are so real! You're adventurous.
> A Bohemian! You confront life as though it
> wasn't – well – terrifying.

JUNE pours brandy into two glasses.

> **JUNE**
>
> How on earth can I expect you to want to share your life with someone who earns a living avoiding tax for people who exploit others, and then sneer at them for being losers?

> **FLORIA**
>
> Bugger Bohemia. What I want is for you to do my tax evasion.

> **JUNE**
>
> God, I admire you.

She gives one of the glasses of brandy to FLORIA, and smiles down at her.

ACT TWO

> FLORIA
>
> *(Looks up.)*

What?

> JUNE
>
> Nothing.

> FLORIA
>
> What?

> JUNE
>
> I like looking at you.

FLORIA pulls a face.

> JUNE
>
> You're such a sensuous woman...

> FLORIA
>
> Oh, sure.

> JUNE
>
> You need warmth... light... colour. Exotic surroundings...

FLORIA picks up a magazine, and begins to turn the pages. JUNE leans against the bookcase, contemplating her, glass in hand.

> JUNE
>
> The setting? A pleasantly furnished apartment somewhere in Bayswater.

> FLORIA
>
> Bayswater?

> JUNE
>
> Highgate?

> FLORIA
>
> Hackney. Dernier cri.

JUNE

Hackney. The odd mellow antique ... a fine oil painting ...

FLORIA

You wish.

JUNE

Persian rugs – their colours faded by years of sunlight.
And the sofa ... what secrets could those silken cushions not reveal? What – he asked himself, as he savoured the subtly feminine atmosphere, the flavour of something withheld, something devious even – of this dark-eyed, maroon crystal of a woman ... What could those shy, faded roses not betray if ...

FLORIA turns a page.

JUNE

She turns a page. White hand on the dusky leather, hair loose, silky gown alive in the firelight, her mouth parted slightly as she pants, despite herself, at the fiery force of the story – by the strange compulsion of the tale. His tale. Written in the hard, white hills of the Extramadura during that long, hot summer ...

FLORIA leaps up and knocks her sideways, to search in a drawer of the desk.

JUNE

What?!

FLORIA

Where the fuck are they?

JUNE

What?

ACT TWO

FLORIA

The batteries for the tape recorder!

JUNE

I've no idea.

FLORIA

Why didn't I think of it before?

JUNE

What?

FLORIA

Novels!

JUNE

I beg your pardon?

FLORIA

I should write novels!

JUNE

What?

FLORIA

Figure it out! No sodding directors. No moody, bloody musicians rapping on about money. All I need is a publisher. And an editor to sort out the text.

JUNE

Are you sure?

FLORIA

Of course, I'm sure. We've cracked it? Orange Prize, Booker Prize, film rights – the residuals alone will pay for our trips to Venice – and we'll lay those off as research. It's a doddle. No funding nightmares – having to arse-lick bloody producers. What a fucking great idea. God, I'm good!

JUNE

Does this mean you'll be staying?

FLORIA

We need to check it out. Find a hole in the market. Look at Bridget Jones. Harry Potter. That guy is loaded! He's writing one a year for the next twenty years.

JUNE

So, I won't need to sell the house?

FLORIA

We must get the right software ... What? (*Clicks her fingers.*) Say it again.

JUNE

I won't have to sell the house.

FLORIA

No! That crap you were on about – a man and a woman
– batteries!

She storms off. JUNE is transfixed.

Light change.

Loud, triumphant MUSIC from RAY.

ACT TWO SCENE TWO

JUNE on the sofa, in new, comfortable clothes, writing on a yellow pad. FLORIA, on her mobile, calls across to her.

FLORIA

Amy's knifed her husband.

ACT TWO

JUNE nods, not hearing.

> **FLORIA**
> (*Into phone*)
> Yeah? (*To JUNE*) She said she didn't mind her in the bedroom but she wasn't having his slut in her kitchen. (*Into phone.*) Don't worry, Amy, you'll be fine. Inez says you've got Neptune ascending ... Stay cool ... Ciao. (*She rings off. To JUNE:*) We're out of coffee.

JUNE works away, un-hearing.

FLORIA reads from a bound manuscript.

> **FLORIA**
> "They followed the sound. At the bottom of the gorge there lay a deer, a young doe. She turned to him. "Is it dead?" He said: "I think so," and leapt down, holding branches, and sliding down the gully. She followed him slowly and when she reached the bottom, he was bending over the animal and she saw that it was alive. He knelt, and there was something about the bend of his neck, something unprotected. She felt a clutch of tenderness. A rush of feeling so strong that she found herself stepping back, to be safe; to be inoculated from something dangerous, out of her control. He looked up at her, then lifted the animal in his arms and began to climb."

They look across the table at each other.

> **FLORIA**
> It needs to go faster.

Light change.

MUSIC.

ACT TWO SCENE THREE

FLORIA is on the sofa.

JUNE enters, waves, puts down her briefcase, exits, and returns without her coat. She flops down in a chair.

JUNE

God! They say policemen think everybody's a crook. They should talk to accountants! I am bushed. Three hours across the desk from a fraudster with bad breath ... Oh! I forgot to shop. I'll ring for a takeaway. (*To FLORIA*) Chinese? Curry? Fish and chips? Are you all right? Floria, what's the matter?

She takes the letter from FLORIA's hand, and reads it.

They gaze at each other.

MUSIC.

ACT TWO SCENE FOUR

JUNE is combing FLORIA's hair.

JUNE

(*Dreamy*)

Is it really true?

She puts an arm around FLORIA.

FLORIA

This is the happiest day of my life.

They sit, arms around each other.

ACT TWO

JUNE

Would you like me to come with you?

FLORIA

Where?

JUNE

To the meeting.

FLORIA

No. I'll look more vulnerable on my own.

JUNE laughs.

FLORIA

In the silk Chalayan I will.

JUNE

Not the Nicole Fahri?

FLORIA

No. That would give the game away.

JUNE

I agree. I don't know what you mean, but I agree.

FLORIA throws a cushion at her. They have a cushion fight.

JUNE stops.

JUNE

Darling. You can't take that meeting. Not without protection. You must get an agent at once.

FLORIA

Already sorted. I'm with Morvenna Friedel. Ace Yank. Great clients both sides of the pond.

JUNE

Why didn't you tell me?

FLORIA

Need to know.

JUNE

What does that mean? What do you mean?

FLORIA

I wanted to get everything in place. Surprise you.
What's the matter?

JUNE

Nothing. I'm surprised you didn't tell me, that's all.
What time is the meeting?

Light change.

MUSIC.

ACT TWO SCENE FIVE

JUNE is standing. She's on her mobile.

JUNE

We can't believe it! The first publisher we showed
it to! ... I know ... I'd no idea new writers could get
such a huge advance! Obviously, they think it will be
a best-seller. I can't believe it, Inez! I've been making
passion-fruit ice-cream. Dreadful fuss but she likes
it. I've even bought caviar! ... I will, Inez, I will. We'll
celebrate. 'Bye.

She rings off and exits. She returns with a bowl of flowers. Then
she opens the large silver cigarette box, and fills it with cigarettes.
She exits. FLORIA enters, dressed to die for. JUNE enters with a
large tray of food.

ACT TWO

JUNE

Tara! Ce soir, madame, we have caviar a la Melba toast, petit poisson and ... passion fruit ice-cream!

FLORIA

Can't. I'm going out.

She crosses and exits. JUNE sits. She picks up a piece of toast, takes a bite, and puts it down. She lights up a cigarette. She is a non-smoker. Offstage, a RADIO is switched on. The SOUND of a DEEJAY – followed by the song "ANYTHING GOES." It is switched off, and FLORIA enters in a silver dress and vestigial sandals.

FLORIA

What do you think?

JUNE lifts up her arms.

FLORIA

Twelve hundred smackers.

FLORIA scoffs some of the food.

FLORIA

Mmm! Save it. I'll have it later.

She goes.

JUNE picks up the piece of toast, then puts it down again.

She tries the cigarette again, then stubs it out.

MUSIC.

ACT TWO SCENE SIX

JUNE crosses in her underwear, and exits. She returns in an elegant dress, with a small hat and a red clutch bag.

FLORIA enters, looking sensational.

> **JUNE**
> *(Nervous)*
How do I look?

> **FLORIA**
> *(Holding two scarves.)*
Great. Should I have this or this?

JUNE chooses. FLORA throws the other one round her neck.

> **FLORIA**
Are my seams straight?

> **JUNE**
I thought you were going to wear the aquamarines.

> **FLORIA**
What?

> **JUNE**
Never mind.

> **FLORIA**
Do I look the business?

> **JUNE**
> *(French pronunciation)*
Formidable.

> **FLORIA**
And feisty.

> **JUNE**
Absolutely.

> **FLORIA**
Like Ian McEwan with balls.

ACT TWO

JUNE
You've never read Ian McEwan.

FLORIA
You've never read Jackie Collins. Best plots in the business. Get off the bike, June. I'm telling you: literary is passé.

She goes. JUNE follows.

MUSIC.

ACT TWO SCENE SEVEN

JUNE enters supporting FLORIA, who sits heavily. JUNE lifts her feet onto the sofa. FLORIA lies back.

FLORIA
Zizi!

She throws her long scarf at JUNE, who dances, singing.

FLORIA
Yeah. How about that!

JUNE
So many celebrities!

FLORIA
And Michael Portillo.

JUNE
They do have a very good list.

FLORIA
Get the right publisher, you can't go wrong.

JUNE

Absolutely.

FLORIA

You didn't mind that I called you my cousin?

JUNE

Of course not.

JUNE crosses, puts on some MUSIC. "SMOKE GETS IN YOUR EYES." They dance with FLORIA's head on JUNE's shoulder.

JUNE

Tired?

FLORIA

Yeah...

But they dance.

JUNE

Shall we dance forever?

FLORIA

Yeah.

MUSIC.

ACT TWO SCENE EIGHT

FLORIA is on her mobile.

FLORIA

...I can't. No, I said I can't... Because, for one thing, my bloody hand has seized up from signing books... We're top of the list. Why do I need to keep selling? For the last six months I've been on the road! I need a break! B-r-a-k-e... What? Let me make this simple.

ACT TWO

I am taking off. Now. For my sanity's sake ... Oh, sod off!

JUNE enters, in trainers and jeans from running.

FLORIA

Bloody publishers! I make a fortune for them. Do they get their act together?

JUNE

Tea, coffee – gin?

FLORIA

Brandy.

JUNE pours.

JUNE

To you.

FLORIA

To me.

They drink.

FLORIA

The word gratitude does not exist. They see me and they see dollar signs.

JUNE

Where did they want you to go?

FLORIA

Turkey. Literary convention. Who's the name?
Me. Carrying the whole bloody pageant on my back.

JUNE

You're tired. You need a holiday. I watch you giving out to people ... You're shredded, darling. You need a holiday.

FLORIA does not answer.

> **JUNE**
> I'll fix it. Where would you like to go? Maldives? Martinique? Of course! Venice! We can do it, at last. See the Titians, the Tintorettos. Be devils – stay at the Danieli.

> **FLORIA**
> The Cipriani. I've already booked.

> **JUNE**
> Floria! You angel! You're wicked. You didn't say a word. I shall be slaughtered. We're in the middle of contracts. Oh, to hell with them! Venice! You did say Venice? The Cipriani. Is that the hotel on the Lido?

> **FLORIA**
> Yeah. Leaving tomorrow.

> **JUNE**
> You're not serious. We can't possibly leave tomorrow.

> **FLORIA**
> Not you. Me.

> **JUNE**
> You mean, alone? You're going alone?

> **FLORIA**
> With some other people. And Inez.

> **JUNE**
> Inez?

JUNE takes a cigarette out of the cigarette box and lights it.

> **JUNE**
> You might have told me.

ACT TWO

Light change.

MUSIC.

ACT TWO SCENE NINE

JUNE, in her bathrobe, is on the telephone.

JUNE

What you have to understand, Dudley, is that there is somebody for everyone. There is someone out there for a kind man with a sense of humour. I'd go for you myself, if I wasn't gay ... Don't be on trial all the time. Put the world on trial. Your world – the world you make ... It's simple. Just say to yourself: 'What do I want?' ... Exactly. And then go for it. And, if you get a No, laugh and say: 'You can't blame me for trying. You're special.' ... Yes, yes, get out there. Put a tissue in your pocket for any egg on your face ... Exactly. The same as everybody else. It's your privilege and responsibility to look out for yourself ... Yes. Get out there! ... Okay, thanks ... And to you. 'Bye!

She puts down the telephone.

JUNE

Oh God. Telling him how to do it! What the fuck do I know?

Light change.

MUSIC.

ACT TWO SCENE TEN

JUNE, in her work clothes, has just returned from the office and sits, hunched, smoking a cigarette, and listening to *Tristan and Isolde* on the RADIO. She looks up. FLORIA has entered.

JUNE

(*Turning off the radio.*)

Floria! I didn't hear you come in! How was it? You're so brown! Was it as wonderful as we dreamed?

FLORIA

Great. We stopped off in Rome and Paris for the collections.

She hands JUNE a big package.

FLORIA

Here. For you.

JUNE unwraps it. It is a large, mauve glass vase.

JUNE

Thanks.

FLORIA

Murano glass. Locally blown. It was hell getting it back. The PR never stopped complaining.

JUNE

Thanks.

She holds the vase, eventually finding a place for it.

An uncomfortable pause.

JUNE

I've finished painting the kitchen. It looks twice as big and three times as light. (*Pause*) And the book's still at number four!

ACT TWO

FLORIA

It's back at number three.

JUNE

Good! What about the paperback?

FLORIA

All sorted.

Silence.

JUNE picks up the silver box and offers FLORIA a cigarette.

FLORIA

I've given up.

JUNE

You've given up smoking?!

Amazed, she lights one for herself.

FLORIA

It's bad for you.

JUNE

And not where it's at.

FLORIA

What's that supposed to mean?

JUNE

Nothing. I've stopped trying to discover what's in and what's out. Not eating, and drinking a lot of water seem to be in.

Silence.

JUNE

I'll go and unpack for you.

FLORIA

My stuff's not here.

JUNE

Oh, Floria! They haven't lost it!

FLORIA

I'm at the Ritz.

JUNE

Why? What's happening?

FLORIA

I'm moving into a loft with Inez. It's not ready yet.
(*Of cigarette box*) Leave that. 'I'm taking it with me.

FLORIA takes the cigarette box.

JUNE

Moving? Permanently? You're leaving?

FLORIA

Have to. I can't stay here.

JUNE

You're leaving me?

FLORIA

You know the saying . . .

JUNE

"Don't do anything for too damn long." Hemingway.

FLORIA

"Keep on trucking." Robert Crumb.

JUNE

(*Puzzled.*)

You're leaving me.

ACT TWO

FLORIA

I'll sort out anything decent. Inez, or her PA, will pick it up. You're welcome to what's left.

JUNE

Inez has a loft? And a PA? I thought she was broke.

FLORIA

Au contraire. She's flying.

JUNE

Doing what?

FLORIA

Running a dungeon.

JUNE sits.

FLORIA

I have to go now. I'm seeing my publisher. Enjoy the vase.

FLORIA goes. JUNE sits for a long moment.

Light change.

MUSIC.

ACT TWO SCENE ELEVEN

JUNE appears in FLORIA's dreadful old dressing gown.

She is smoking. She wanders about.

The TELEPHONE rings. She picks it up.

JUNE

No, she's not here.

She puts the phone down, and smokes.

The TELEPHONE rings again. She picks it up, and puts it straight down again. She stands, thinking, then dials a number.

JUNE
Hullo Ruth? It's June. I won't be in today ... No. If you need any information speak to Harriet.

She rings off, and stands, immobile.

Light change.

MUSIC.

ACT TWO SCENE ELEVEN

JUNE, in pyjamas, is listening to the RADIO.

INTERVIEWER
And now ... the first winner of the new Atalanta Literary Prize. Floria de Winter!

FLORIA
Thank you for having me.

INTERVIEWER
This has been a momentous year for you. This is the second prize you've won ...

FLORIA
Third actually.

INTERVIEWER
Of course! You won the De Beauvoir! Were you surprised? I mean, the French are so famously chauvinistic.

ACT TWO

FLORIA

Pas de tout. They gave me a wonderful dinner at the George Cinq. And, of course, meeting Depardieu was to die for.

INTERVIEWER

We saw the pictures! It's amazing, the way your character, Rose, has become such an icon. A model for the feminine woman in a genderless world. Wasn't that how you put it?

FLORIA

Look. We are mammals. Tribal. We gravitate to one another naturally. I mean, at its worst, it's racism, but we have to accept a sort of basic – how shall I say – isness.

INTERVIEWER

I think I see what you mean.

FLORIA

We cleave together. We're no good on our own. The woman in my book – of course she wants equal footing in the world – not only with men but with people of different ages, class, nationality ...

JUNE

I said that!

FLORIA

What she doesn't need is a sort of attenuated, isolated life where she yaws between a natural desire to breed and nurture, and the demands of her cortex. Her thinking, achieving self.

JUNE

I said that!

FLORIA
What she fears. What Rose suffers. What women dread – what we all dread – is to be alone.

JUNE switches off the radio, and sits immobile.

A burst of MUSIC from RAY. It is GOTTERDAMMERUNG.

JUNE rises to thump on the wall, but changes her mind. She returns to the RADIO, switches it on, tunes it to Radio 3 and the Wagner – very loud.

MUSIC.

ACT TWO SCENE TWELVE

The DOORBELL rings. JUNE, scruffy in an old top and trousers, rears up, half-awake, from the sofa. FLORIA enters.

FLORIA
I let myself in. My God, what's happened to you?

JUNE gapes at FLORIA, who looks really stunning now.

JUNE
What's happened to you?

FLORIA
Mini-lift. Botox. Macrobiotic and Pilates.

JUNE
I believe you. Well, except for the macrobiotic.

FLORIA
I have a private food trainer. You have to get the vanity/greed balance in sync. You should try it.

ACT TWO

JUNE

What do you want?

FLORIA

I was passing.

JUNE

In Wimbledon?

FLORIA

An old friend is always worth the detour. Why aren't you at work?

JUNE

Ah! You thought I'd be out. You called thinking I'd be out.

FLORIA

Channel 4 want to do a piece on me. They want to film here, where the book was written.

JUNE

No.

MUSIC.

ACT TWO SCENE THIRTEEN

JUNE is sitting. FLORIA pours tea from a pot.

She gives a cup to JUNE.

FLORIA

Biscuit?

JUNE shakes her head. FLORIA helps herself.

FLORIA

God, these are stale! (*She takes another.*) You look dreadful.

JUNE

I've been ill.

FLORIA

What with?

JUNE

They're not sure.

FLORIA

Not catching, I hope. What's it called?

JUNE

Bi-polar schizotypal affective disorder.

FLORIA

Is that that yuppie thing where you're bushed all the time? I thought that was out of fashion now.
More tea?

JUNE shakes her head.

FLORIA

How did you get it? Is it painful?

JUNE doesn't answer. FLORA leans forward, forcing a reply.

JUNE

I was in the office one morning. I don't know. All of a sudden, someone pushed a Hoover in the room and sucked all the air out.

FLORIA

Ah. Panic attack.

ACT TWO

JUNE
Even the sounds – the colours went different.

FLORIA
Crikey. What did you do?

JUNE
Got up and left.

FLORIA
Where to?

JUNE
(Shakes her head.)
Little Venice. By the canal.

FLORIA
Water's good for stress. What then?

JUNE
I looked at the houseboats.

FLORIA
And?

JUNE
Threw my handbag in.

FLORIA
In the canal? With your credit cards?

JUNE
And my cheque book.

FLORIA
How did you get them out?

JUNE
I didn't. They sank.

FLORIA

Christ.

JUNE

Then I went out on to the Westway flyover.

FLORIA

What for?

JUNE

Don't know. I just walked out into the road and sat down.

FLORIA

In the middle of the traffic?

JUNE

Yes.

FLORIA

Were you killed?

This gets a small smile from JUNE.

JUNE

No, but a lorry driver beat me up.

FLORIA

Did you sue?

JUNE

Floria, it was my fault. I bent his lorry.

Silence.

JUNE

I've been let go. By the company.

FLORIA

If we film here, they'll pay you a fee. They'll pay something.

ACT TWO

JUNE

I was in a clinic. For depression. In France, they call it "amertume." Bitterness. (*Slight pause.*) So, what about you?

FLORIA

Just finalised the American paperback deal. Amazing.

JUNE

That's good.

FLORIA

And we've sold the film rights.

JUNE

For how much?

FLORIA

Two million dollars. It's awesome. Look, if you need a hand-out ...

She takes out her cheque book and writes a cheque. JUNE watches her. She holds the cheque out to JUNE, who leans forward and reads the amount.

JUNE

Five thousand.

She takes the cheque, tears it in half, and hands it back.

JUNE

I did it for you.

FLORIA

That was the arrangement. (*Pause.*) So, no hard feelings?

JUNE

I didn't say that.

FLORIA

Oh, you mean you didn't do it for me? It was a deal?
Well, tough tit. Look, June, success is not your scene.
You'd never handle the stress. The moment I'm not
around to babysit, you'd have a breakdown.

JUNE punches FLORIA to the ground. She then helps her to her feet, and picks up her hat.

FLORIA

What was that for? You're obviously up shit creek.
Take the five thousand! How much do you want?

JUNE

Nothing. I don't want anything from you.

FLORIA backs off warily.

JUNE

It's all right. You've nothing to reproach yourself for.

FLORIA

Absolutely. It wasn't my idea.

JUNE

No, it wasn't. It was mine. You owe me nothing. What
you gave me was priceless. Incomparable. You gave
me a life.

She closes on FLORIA, and gazes at her face.

JUNE

Can one expect an eagle to be thoughtful?

She dusts FLORIA's hat off across her leg, and hands it back.

ACT TWO

JUNE

Nice hat.

FLORIA

Look, if you want ...

But JUNE stares at her steadily, and FLORIA goes. JUNE looks after her thoughtfully, then begins to prowl up and down.

> *Light change.*

MUSIC.

ACT TWO SCENE FOURTEEN

JUNE comes in from jogging. She throws off her sweatshirt, and exits. Then she returns with a yoga mat. She does some yoga, then rises, crosses to the wall, and pounds on it.

JUNE

Ray! Music!

We hear hoarse shouting from RAY, next-door.

JUNE

Anything!

Loud WAGNER MUSIC from RAY. JUNE thinks, realising she is sweaty, and exits. The WAGNER becomes triumphant.

JUNE enters, in a clean shirt, and trousers. She crosses and, from a drawer in the bookcase, she gets out a pile of yellow pads. She makes herself comfortable on the sofa, and starts writing.

> *Light change.*

MUSIC changes to Bostridge singing SCHUBERT.

ACT TWO SCENE FIFTEEN

SCHUBERT MUSIC continues.

JUNE, on the sofa, stops writing for a moment to put on a cardigan. Then she continues working. She pauses to listen to the music from next door. Then she goes back to work. The DOORBELL RINGS.

JUNE ignores it.

MUSIC changes to Maria Callas singing in LA TRAVIATA.

ACT TWO SCENE SIXTEEN

LA TRAVIATA MUSIC continues.

JUNE is at the table working – filling the yellow legal pads.

The MUSIC from next door changes to IT WAS JUST ONE OF THOSE THINGS, to THE TRUMPET VOLUNTARY, to I'LL GET BY.

At each change of music, JUNE takes another position to work: from the table, to a chair, to the sofa.

MUSIC: the pas de deux from NUTCRACKER.

JUNE collates the pages she has written – a thick wedge – and puts them into a box-file.

Light change.

ACT TWO SCENE SEVENTEEN

The MUSIC fades out as VOICES are heard offstage.

ACT TWO

JUNE

(Offstage)

Thanks, Ray!

JUNE enters, looking good.

JUNE

(Calls at the door)

The snails were great!

She throws off her coat, loosens her belt, and pats her stomach, laughing. The DOORBELL rings. She lets it ring. Then goes to answer it. FLORIA enters, followed by JUNE. FLORIA looks a mess. She has put on weight.

FLORIA

I've been trying to reach you.

JUNE

So I gather. I'm out a lot of the time.

FLORIA

Doing what?

JUNE

This and that.

FLORIA

Didn't Inez get in touch?

JUNE

And Sonya. And Jeremy.

FLORIA

That prick. You got my messages?

JUNE

Yes.

FLORIA

Then why haven't you ... ?

JUNE

Floria, what do you want?

FLORIA

You know what I want. (*Pause.*) You said you did it for me! So ... ? (*Pause.*) Please! I'll do anything. Just say what you want.

JUNE

Don't.

FLORIA

What?

JUNE

Don't piddle all over my floor.

FLORIA

I'm desperate.

JUNE

But that's no good. I can't deal with that. Either you're a diva or ... God, is this my fault? Have I turned you into this?

FLORIA

Look, I know I'm a shit. I'm Mr Toad. But I got carried away. What did you expect, June? You know me. You know I'm a chancer. How could I know the book was going to be such a bloody success? It was just another scam, like the others. But this was something else. New territory. There was no way I could have a literary life in Wimbledon, and how could I ask you to uproot yourself? This is your home.

ACT TWO

JUNE

Oh, you're good.

FLORIA

Yes, I know. I'm doing it again. But what else can I do?
It's kill or be killed out there. If you'd had my fucking
family! Shoved off by my mother. No father.
A sister I never knew ...

JUNE

Shut up! Floria, you have a perfectly good family.
Your father's a wholesale grain merchant in Hull.
Your mother's a pillar of the community. You have
two sisters – one married to a dentist – the other a
sales manager in Bury St Edmunds. And a brother
in the shoe business who likes golf and wind-surfing.
Your parents have been married for forty years. Your
second sister's husband has an OBE for services above
the call of duty to the fire service, and your real name
is Frances Bickerstaff.

Silence.

FLORIA

So, will you do it?

JUNE

Yes.

FLORIA

Yes?

JUNE

I'll do it.

FLORIA

You mean it?

JUNE

Yes.

FLORIA

Ohhh! (*She knocks over a chair.*) I didn't know what to do, Junie. I spent eighteen months ... eighteen months on that sequel!

JUNE

Well, never mind. (*Rights the chair.*)

FLORIA

What do you mean never mind? It was eighteen months of my life! I couldn't believe them, why they turned it down.

JUNE

Perhaps they were thrown by the change of style.

FLORIA

That's what I mean!

JUNE

Floria, I've said I'll do it.

FLORIA

How long?

JUNE

Sorry?

FLORIA

How long will it take you to write it?

JUNE

I've no idea.

FLORIA

Two months – three months – six?

ACT TWO

JUNE

I don't know. I shall need somewhere to work for a start, I can't work here.

FLORIA

Why not? You did before.

Silence.

FLORIA

What about my place in Highgate? Super views, there's a sauna on the roof.

JUNE

No-o. Not London. I need somewhere ...
Somewhere ... I need to be inspired.

FLORIA

Abroad then. Rome, Paris, Morocco ...

JUNE

On my own? I'd be lonely.

FLORIA

(Small.)

I could come with you. Where would you like to go?
I know – Venice! You've always wanted to see Venice.
You love Venice!

JUNE

(Muses.)

Venice ... Venice ... Ye-es ... Venice might do it for me.

FLORIA

We'll rent a palazzo on the Grand Canal, for however long you want – near St Mark's Square – not the Lido, it's naff. A palazzo, by the Academia.

JUNE

All right.

FLORIA

Great. Fantastic.

JUNE

We'll draw up a contract. Fifty-fifty.

Silence.

FLORIA

I got it together. You'd never have got it together.

JUNE

Fifty-fifty.

FLORIA

You've thought this out.

JUNE

I have.

FLORIA

You said you didn't care about money.

JUNE

Oh, I didn't say that. (*She gets a drink.*) A deal?

FLORIA

I have a lot of expenses.

JUNE

I'm looking forward to the same.

She clinks her glass against FLORIA's, then settles back on the sofa.

JUNE

You know what I'm going to enjoy most?

ACT TWO

FLORIA

(Sulky.)

I don't know. Travel? Books?

JUNE

Really expensive shoes.

They relax.

FLORIA

I've been thinking film scripts, but it's better to write the novels, sell the rights, and let the hacks do the screenplays. (*Pause.*) I did have one idea for a film, though.

JUNE turns to her.

FLORIA

Joan the Musical.

THE END.

Also from Quota Books . . .

PAM GEMS
Plays One

**THE INCORRUPTIBLE
GARIBALDI, SI
THE TREAT**

*

PAM GEMS
Plays Two

**BETTY'S WONDERFUL CHRISTMAS
THE SOCIALISTS
GUINEVERE
ETHEL**

Q

AVAILABLE FROM: WWW.QUOTABOOKS.COM

MARS ATTACKS MEMOIRS
By Mila Pop

Reviews

A rare insight into the Tim Burton cult classic. Hear about Hollywood behind the scenes and the development of the Mars Attacks! movie. A must read for movie buffs and fans alike.

LUKE ETTENSPERGER

The Mini-Cooper of the literary world, this book is nippy and stylish, attentive to detail, with a disarming, quirky exterior that belies a deep intelligence and timeless design. Mila Pop is a great interviewer; her questions, as well as her delight at the responses Gems provides, show that she clearly loves the film. Jonathan Gems answers her questions generously and on many levels. He explains how the movie almost did not come about (the phrase 'madcap adventure' comes to mind) and offers funny and fascinating anecdotes about some of the people involved. He also gives us the inside skinny on how the film industry and Hollywood really work, and from there goes into how this paradigm can be seen throughout society. His great affection for Tim Burton and his girlfriend, Lisa-Marie, is very touching and transcends mere artistic collaboration. The book nails the sense of a collection of supremely talented people having a blast as they create unique and wonderful things – namely the movie itself, the friendships made along the way, and the interaction between Pop and Gems. It's an easy, happy read, over all too quickly. I look forward to more.

LEELA MILLER

A fantastic fun read. You will not be disappointed. It's like sitting on a couch with both Jonathan and Mila and hearing awesome stories on how a movie is written and put together.

PATRICK EVRARD.

I am so glad I bought this book 'cause I almost didn't after seeing the cover. Now I know the meaning of 'Never judge a book by its cover!' This is the book everyone needs to read. Our education and society would be so much better if this book was part of the school syllabus. It's very subversive and incredibly intelligent. Criticizes everything wrong with today's society and offers solutions. Unbelievable story, unbelievable writing. If I had to choose one book to read through eternity, this would be the one!

JOSH on AMAZON.CO.UK

Full of anecdotes about the film, its star-studded cast, the writer and director, and their struggles with the suited executives. Every page has a jewel to throw light upon the people behind the movies we love. Want to know what goes on behind the scenes in Hollywood? Here we see exactly what creatives go through to see their ideas brought to life by the mega-corporations. If you've ever seen Mars Attacks you will absolutely love this book.

WILLIAM HARWARD.

I found it fascinating that he and Tim Burton were able to take so many risks in this modern era of conglomerate films. His comments are a refreshing insight into a Hollywood which is in desperate need of being spruced up.

JUDE ZIETARA.

In Europe and South America, movies are called 'The Seventh Art.' In the USA, they are called 'The Industry.' After reading this insightful, funny, and sometimes shocking, book, I can see why.

MILANKO LUKOVIC.

A fascinating read about scriptwriting and filmmaking. I never knew how interesting the whole process was, and I enjoyed getting to know the stars and the crew. I was laughing all the way through.

COLIN PANRUCKER.

Mila Pop's lively and natural passion for people and their lives is infectious and fun. It will always leave you wanting more. The wacky Mars Attacks! is like nothing else, and so the wacky and hectic story of how it got made is fitting. The very touch-and-go nature of the movie industry is revealed. It can turn on a dime from gushing praise and promise to frozen over and aloof. Aspiring writers, directors, and actors take note! In Jonathan Gems, we see a man sustained by gratitude and the company of good people, self-possessed and of great calibre. Fully aware of others and soaking up the details of life. A true writer. He shows us that under all of the urgent and overblown dramatics and bravado of big movie-making are real people – flawed and brilliant. Generous with his many stories, you will likewise be left wanting more.

RO HACKETT

So very interesting getting new insights into the world of film and show business. What a clever man Jonathan Gems is too. So well read. I want to see the film again to pick up on all the extra things we now know.

DENNIS PIERCE.

This guy is amazing. He tries to tell you how we have no say or power when it comes to movies because of controlling rich people. Jonathan Gems you're my hero. Jonathan was trying to get out to the people that art is being held hostage.

TYLER on AMAZON.COM

WHO KILLED BRITISH CINEMA?
By Vinod Mahindru and Jonathan Gems

Reviews

Who killed British cinema? It's a good question – especially since us Brits used to have the second biggest film industry in the world and now it is practically non-existent. And the question gets explored with real vigour in this interesting and well put-together book.

It brings forth a mix of opinions whilst examining theories that could very well explain the 'death' of British cinema.

Not only is it refreshingly honest, but it is also very detailed, as it is richly supported by intriguing stats and thought-provoking quotes from credible individuals from the film industry (taken from pre-arranged interviews). Because of this, there is real insight within the copy and, as it has been thoroughly researched, you can find out more about the history of British cinema and its unfortunate decline in a succinct way. You don't have to pore over lengthy textbooks or wordy theories to grasp the timeline of events.

Overall, this makes for a riveting read that unpicks the political and cultural factors influencing media production and development over the decades and, if you are a film buff, you will particularly enjoy this in-depth piece of non-fiction. It even comes with a list of must-see British films!

HANNAH MONTGOMERY
www.whatson.guide

★★★★★ 5.0 out of 5 stars. **A Film Maker's Must Read!**

There is no shortage of resources for new and emerging filmmakers. There are courses, free and paid apps, some excellent and some not-so-good; there are many, many books written about every aspect of the art, from writing the script to where to stay in Cannes when you're sending your new baby out into a world of adoring soon-to-be fans. All of these, to a greater or lesser degree, have their uses but if, like me, you are involved in the production of shorts and /or features in the UK, there is one resource that will make you angry. Very angry. A book (and documentary film) that will make your blood boil and – if you're anything like me – wonder why you decided to become involved in the obviously pointless world of UK film making in the first place.

If it doesn't make you angry; if it doesn't make you want to scream in rage; if it doesn't make you say: "This has ALL got to change!" then you'd better go and do something else because, believe you me, you might think you love film and cinema, but you most certainly don't!

The book *Who Killed British Cinema?* by Vinod Mahindru and Jonathan Gems, is an in-depth and comprehensive look at the British film industry – or rather, the lack of it – from its glory days when it was the second largest in the world to the present day where there is not one single British movie studio, and 98% of the films in our cinemas are made by foreign entities.

Now don't get me wrong, I'm certainly not a xenophobic Brexiteer Little Englander who thinks everything 'foreign' is bad; far from it. I'm a Remainer who has spent many years of his creative life in Europe, who loves the cinema of Bergman, Fassbinder (Rainer Werner rather than Michael) and Truffaut, but who also grew up with – and has deeply rooted in his soul – the magnificent films of Michael Powell, Emeric Pressburger, Alberto Cavalcanti, Charles Crichton and David Lean – not to mention Terence Davies, Derek Jarman and Peter Greenaway. Films that truly express our national identity; what it means to be British with all its peculiar sensibilities. Films that show our individualities and uniqueness in a way that the current diet of pap served up at the multiplexes could never hope to achieve.

The book examines the way in which film funding has gone in this country. The role of such bodies as the BFI, BAFTA, the erstwhile

Regional Screen Agencies, Creative England and, most interestingly, the policy of successive governments that have led to the demise of our most successful creative industry.

Read it. Watch the documentary. Listen to what the ex-CEO's of these august bodies say about spending 65% of their agency's budget not on film production but on admin and salaries. Read about funding bodies that fund production companies owned by members of the funding bodies who granted the funds in the first place. Do this and don't get mad, I dare you!

This is not a negative book, nor a negative film. It is rather a call to arms for every filmmaker in the UK to say: "This is not right. This has to change."

I found it inspirational. I found that, though my blood boiled at the sheer injustice of it all, it has increased my determination to succeed ten-fold. As Buckminster Fuller is quoted at the end of the documentary film: "You never change things by fighting the existing reality. To change something, build a new model that makes the existing model obsolete."

If you buy one book about filmmaking, let it be this one. It will change your life and, who knows? maybe just help you to reinvent our beloved industry.

IAN MCLAUGHLIN MBKS

Q

website: www.quotabooks.com
email: info@quotabooks.com
Twitter: @Quotabooks

www.ingramcontent.com/pod-product-compliance
Lightning Source LLC
Chambersburg PA
CBHW072044110526
44590CB00018B/3033